"CALVINISM"
THE TROJAN HORSE WITHIN

This booklet is written to those who have not become ensnared in the heresies of Augustinianism/Calvinism, as a firewall of protection against possibly one of the worst heresies in church history. Calvinism is "another gospel" and needs to be rooted out of our Biblically sound churches. Remember "Uzzah".

by: Terry Lee Miller Sr.

"Calvinism" The Trojan Horse Within
Copyright © 2008 by Terry Lee Miller Sr.

Eternity Publications
1252 Sessions Road, Elgin SC 29045
(803) 438-4405

Printed in the United States of America

ISBN 978-1-7350281-0-1 (paperback)
978-1-7350281-2-5 (ebook)

All rights reserved solely by the author. The author guarantees all contents are original and do not infringe upon the legal rights of any other person or work. No part of this book may be reproduced in any form without the permission of the author. The views expressed in this book are not necessarily those of the publisher.

Unless otherwise indicated, Bible quotations are taken from The King James Version 1611.

—WARNING CALVINISM VS THE DEITY OF CHRIST—

Calvinism unwittingly brings the doctrine of the deity of Christ into question by inferring that Jesus lied by preaching a false warning, when He preached that one could go to hell forever if he did not repent and believe on Him! Why so? Simple, according to Calvinism no one is "in danger" of going to hell, the elect cannot possibly go there even if presently not saved since they will ultimately surely be saved (so why warn them?), and the non-elect must go to hell since there is no chance of them being saved since they cannot possibly be in "danger" of going there. To "be in danger of going to hell" clearly implies a possibility of not having to go there, which the "non-elect" do not have (according to Calvinism). Thus according to Calvin, no one is in danger of going to hell! To say that since we do not know who is elect and who is not, therefore we should preach such warning, still is to be preaching a false lying warning (if one believes Calvinism)! If our Savior preached a lie, then He sinned and obviously could not have been God! The fact Jesus **DID** preach warnings about the possibility of one going to hell unless he repents, therefore proves Calvinism unwittingly brings the deity of Christ into disrepute. Isn't it amazing that so many Christian leaders, pastors etc, who are not Calvinists, do not regard Calvinism as a serious heresy or threat to Biblical Christianity?

PROCLAIMING

The time has come for we who know and believe the truth to separate ourselves from fellowshipping with calvinists. Therefore this booklet is dedicated to the overthrow and demise of Augustinian / Calvinistic influences in Bible believing churches and schools.

-DISCLAIMER-

WARNING: If you are a Calvinist beware! This booklet exposes serious and distorted false teachings regarding the sovereignty of God, and the Biblical doctrine of election and predestination. It is not written to/for Calvinists since Calvinism generally renders its followers unreachable/unteachable. Since this booklet accurately exposes the heresies of Calvin by print and some few cartoons, the Calvinist reader will be highly offended that his leader's foolish doctrines have been exposed and disproven. Therefore it may be best for Calvinists to avoid reading this publication. Under freedom of religion Calvinists have the full right under the law to estabish their own churches and schools, but for them to infiltrate, take over non-Calvinist churches/schools must be stopped! further it needs to be understood that Calvinsts are taught by their leader to "hide" or "conceal" their divisive doctrines of double predestination etc, which explains why so many Calvinist pastors are able to secretly infiltrate and eventually take over "non-Calvinist" churches! Calvin wrote as follows:

CALVIN'S INSTITUTES CH. 21, BOOK 3:4

I admit that profane men lay hold of the subject of predestination to carp, or cavil, or snarl, or scoff. But if their petulance frightens us, it will be necessary to conceal all the principal articles of faith *(i.e. the T.U.L.I.P. ed.)* because they and their fellows leave scarcely one of them unassailed with blasphemy.

THEREBY CALVINISM THE "TROJAN HORSE" IS ABLE TO ENTER, TAKE OVER, AND CRIPPLE THE CHURCH!

It is the firm opinion of this writer that any pastor/teacher etc. who cannot see the danger of Calvinism entering into a church, especially after reading the following pages, is not qualified to hold teaching/leadership positions in the church, and should be made to resign. It would be well to remember the scripture admonition, Jer. 23:26, They are the prophets of the deceit of their own hearts, and following vs.30, I am against the prophets saith the Lord that steal my words every one from his neighbor. Calvinism does exactly that, it corrupts the simplicity of the gospel in the hearts of young converts! Shun it!

Table of Contents

Chapter One   Calvinism the "Other Gospel" 1

Chapter Two   Fairly Proposing Calvinism 45

Chapter Three   Identification with Calvinism 61

Chapter Four   Proposed Litmus Test 89

Chapter Five   Calvin's Strange Pernicious Theology 103

Chapter Six   Final Thoughts on Augustinian/Calvinism . . 115

Conclusion and Final Notes. 131

Preface

Surely it will be asked, "Why should Calvinism be an issue of debate among Christians since debate in the church severely divides and cripples unity in the body of Christ." The simple answer is that only the true gospel of the Word of God is the power of God unto salvation. Romans 1:16 plainly tells us, "For I am not ashamed of the gospel of Christ, for it is the power of God unto salvation, to the Jew first and also to the Greek." If the true gospel is the power of God unto salvation, then a false gospel is the power of Satan unto damnation! That cannot be refuted. For the first 400 years of church history the church preached and taught only the simple basic truth, that Jesus died for all men, that He offers salvation to all men, that all could be saved, and that we as Christians are to preach the saving gospel to "every creature" then enter the Roman Catholic Bishop of Hippo, Augustine, with the doctrine of pre-election/pre-destination according to the sovereignty of God of only a select few, relegating the rest of humanity to burn in hell fire for eternity, with John Calvin later following in his steps!

We are fast entering a phase in church history where Calvinism has its outstretched tentacles in so many main stream evangelical schools, churches and Christian circles. It is threatening to replace the Biblical gospel with its own perverted gospel making us who know and understand the truth to be the ones preaching a "false gospel."

That the doctrine of "double predestination" **prevents souls from being saved** was clearly brought home to this author many years ago.

As I am a strong personal soul winner, and having been so for over 40 years, I was attempting to win a man to Christ with whom I worked. He was a deacon and Sunday school teacher in a Baptist Church and admitted that he was not, nor ever had been saved. Upon sharing the Romans Road with him and asking him if he wanted to be saved, I was delighted when he told me "Yes" I would like to be saved. To this I suggested that we meet after work at his car so I could further explain the way of salvation. Sitting in his car with him, I told him we could pray together then and there, and he could experience the new birth. To this he simply replied, "Well I cannot do that right now," and when I asked him why he answered as follows. "My church believes in election/Calvinism, and I don't know if I am one of the elect or not, only time will tell if I am." No matter what scripture I showed him, such as "Now is the day of salvation" in Corinthians or Romans 10:13 etc, he simply said… "When the time comes for me to be saved, if I am one of the elect, I will know it!" Therefore the unity or disunity in the body of Christ over Calvinism is certainly not caused by such as this author debating the same, but rather by the false doctrines of Augustinian/Calvinism. Those doctrines are the ones dividing the church and quenching soul winning zeal and fervor and need to be cast out along with those who teach it!

How anyone would dare tamper with the sacred precious plan of salvation, designed and executed by Almighty God! Calvinism certainly does indeed tamper with the plan of salvation, from being that Jesus died for all men, and is the Savior of all men especially of those that believe (1Tim.4:10) and that anyone can be saved, to only a select few are sovereignly elected and can be saved while the rest of the majority are "passed over" in God's secret election and are therefore consigned to burn in hell for eternity!

This author is convinced that when one becomes "infected" with the false doctrines of Calvinism, that there is little hope of recovery. The real reason being when Calvinism is "spoon fed" to an unsuspecting Christian, his simple basic foundation of "salvation is open for all by the death of Christ on the cross" is stripped away, and all scripture is from then on interpreted in the light *(sorry-darkness ed.)* of Calvinistic doctrine as he is indoctrinated.

The Word of God gives a very stern warning to anyone who "adds to or takes away from" sacred inspired scripture. The Calvinist and the Non-Calvinist position on the gospel cannot both be correct, one is certainly a false gospel! It is this author's prayer that these few pages will give the strength needed to help keep these false doctrines out of our doctrinally sound churches, colleges and seminaries. Remember "Uzzah."

ACTS 28:27 …

> For the heart of this people is waxed gross, and their ears are dull of hearing, and their eyes have they closed lest they should see with their eyes, and hear with their heart and should be converted, and I should heal them.

To those who may question why a precious soul is lost, the above scripture is clear that the blame lies not due to a lack of election on God's part, as the Calvinist falsely teach, but rather due to the sinners personal responsibility in refusing to accept the Lord Jesus Christ as personal Savior and Lord. What a strange doctrine it is that wicked ungodly sinful people are eventually saved without their consent as Calvinism teaches. Of course Calvinists say God regenerates them first, (which is still forced salvation), in order to change their desire to eventually be saved. Totally unbiblical!! (This "forced salvation" they piously call "particular redemption.")

The Word of God abounds in warnings to the wicked to turn from their sins or be damned, and always places the full responsibility to be saved or lost squarely on their shoulders, certainly not on the sovereign election of God! Certainly God could be blamed for all the sin and depravity ever committed if Calvinism be true...for if true then God could have elected all to be saved and spared the world of all the sin and depravity it has suffered! Remember Agrippa said to Paul, "Almost thou persuades me to become a Christian." Acts 26:28. The following scripture shows Israel's refusal to come to Christ was not blamed on God's sovereign "non-election" but rather on their own sin and rebellion.

MATT. 23:37...

> O Jerusalem, Jerusalem thou that killest the prophets, and stonest them which are sent unto thee, how often would I have gathered thy children together, even as a hen gathereth her chickens under her wings, and ye would not. *(Not, could not! Ed.)*

Here the Calvinist would have one believe that God, for some "secret" reason, did not "enable" Jerusalem to accept Jesus as their promised Messiah. In the following scripture Calvinism would interpret the text to read as follows:

Preface

JOHN 3:18...

> He that believeth on him is not condemned because God secretly elected him and caused him to believe, but he that believeth not is condemned already because God did not sovereignly elect and cause him to believe and be saved.

To say Calvinism does not attempt to rewrite the Word of God and change its meaning is therefore an understatement! May the Lord rid us of this curse.

"CONTROVERSY"- BY HALDANE

Many religious persons have a dread of controversy and wish truth to be stated without reference to those who hold the opposite errors. Controversy and a bad spirit are, in their estimation, synonymous terms, and strenuously to oppose what is wrong is considered as contrary to Christian meekness. Those who hold this opinion seem to overlook what every page of the New Testament lays before us. In all the history of our Lord Jesus Christ, we never find Him out of controversy. From the moment He entered on the discharge of His office in the synagogue of Nazareth until He expired on the cross, it was an uninterrupted scene of controversy. Nor did He, with all the heavenly meekness which in Him shone so brightly, treat error and truth without a reference to those who held them or study to avoid giving the proper appellation to those corruptions of doctrine or practice that endangered the interests of immortal souls. His censures were not confined to doctrines but included the abettors of false principles themselves.

And as to the apostles, their epistles are generally controversial. Most of them were directly written for the express purpose of vindicating truth and opposing error. The authors of heresies do not escape with an abstract condemnation of their false doctrine. Paul again and again most indignantly denounces the conduct of opposers of the Gospel and by name points out those against whom he cautions his brethren. When Hymenaeus and Alexander erred concerning the faith, and when he delivered them unto Satan that they might learn not to blaspheme he did not compliment them as amiable and learned persons. Even the apostle who treats the subject of love the most and who possessed so much of that spirit which was eminently manifested in the divine Master, does not avoid controversy; nor in controversy does he study to avoid severity of censure on the opposers of the truth. In the examples of opposing truth left on record for our imitation, we perceive nothing of that frigid spirit of indifference which smiles on the corrupters of the Word of God and shuns to call heresy by its proper name. What with holy indignation do the apostles denounce the subtle machinations of the enemies of the Gospel!

In vain shall we look among those faithful servants of the Lord for anything to justify that trembling reserve which fears to say decidedly that truth is truth or that error is error. In what style indeed should perversions of the truth of God be censured? Ought they to be treated as mere matters of opinion on which we may innocently and safely differ? *(Recently this author asked an Independent Baptist Evangelist his opinion on Calvinism. Amazingly with a rather cavalier attitude he said, "Well I think that it is all in a matter of how things are defined." Certainly he saw no real threat in the heresies of Calvin! ed.)* Or ought they to be met in a tone of solemn, strong and decided disapprobation? Paul warned Christians against men who arose from themselves, "speaking perverse things, to draw away disciples after them," and instead of complimenting false teachers in his day, denounced an angel from Heaven on the supposition of his preaching another gospel. And if an apostle was withstood to the face when he was to be blamed, are the writings of those who subvert the Gospel to be passed without rebuke?

While a spirit of lukewarmness and indifference to truth is advancing under the mask of charity and liberality, there is a loud call on all Christians to "stand fast in one spirit, with one mind striving together for the faith of the gospel"; to present a firm and united phalanx of opposition to error under every name, from whatever quarter it may approach; and not to "stumble in their ways from the ancient paths, to walk in paths, in a way not cast up; To make their land desolate" (Jer. 18:15, 16). "Thus saith the Lord, Stand ye in the ways, and see, and ask for the old paths, where is the good way, and walk therein, and ye shall find rest for your souls. But they said, We will not walk therein." (Jer. 6:16). Should believers become unfaithful to their trust and be seduced to abandon their protest against false doctrines, they may gain the approbation of the world, but what will this avail when compared with the favor of God? But if with prayer to God in the use of the appointed means they contend earnestly for the truth, then they may expect the gracious fulfillment of that blessed promise,

> *"When the enemy shall come in like a flood, the Spirit of the Lord shall lift up a standard against him."*
>
> Is. 59:19. (end)

CALVIN'S GOD INTENDED FOR MAN TO SIN

"The first man fell because the Lord deemed it meet that he should:"... "Nor ought it seems absurd when I say, that God not only foresaw the fall of the first man, and in him the ruin of his posterity; but also at his own pleasure arranged it."

by John Calvin: Calvin's Institutes Chapter 23, 3:7&8.

CALVIN'S GOD "CAUSING SOME TO BE SAVED BUT IGNORING THE MAJORITY!?"

Is this the kind of God we have ruling the universe? One who "causes" man to sin and be damned, and then sends him to be tormented in fire and brimstone for eternity? It also naturally follows, if God is the "first cause," then He intended for Lucifer to sin and fall! (Possibly Calvin never said such but he must have believed it!). Notice the next statement by Calvin:

Calvin describes it: "Forever harassed with a dreadful tempest, they shall feel themselves torn asunder by an angry God, and transfixed and penetrated by mortal stings, terrified by the thunderbolts of God, and broken by the weight of this hand, so that to sink into any gulf would be more tolerable than to stand for a moment in these terrors."

The fatal flaw of Calvinism as follows: If the elect were elect from before the foundation of the world due to God's sovereign election of them, then it must be said that the elect were *never* "lost." So when Jesus came to seek and to save the "lost" then only the "non-elect" would qualify for salvation since only they could be said to be "lost" at the time of His incarnation. Thus if only the non-elect were lost at that time and Jesus came to seek and to save that which was lost, then

Preface

Jesus must have saved everyone, the "elect" because they were elected to salvation in eternity past, and as well the "non-elect" since they were the only "lost ones." (Here a perfect example of the unwitting contradicting inferences of Calvinism.)

Reader Note. The author of this booklet is not saying by any means that Calvinists are lost (that some are on both sides of the issue of course is of no doubt). Most Calvinists are recruited to that position after conversion. Most of them do indeed preach the simple gospel of "Believe on the Lord Jesus Christ and thou shalt be saved," but in private and among their theological peers they relish their positions as "Calvinists" and seek to recruit others. Calvinism is a deadly theological virus, especially among new converts. It destroys soul winning zeal, and as well makes God and His supposed "providential decrees" responsible for everything that happens. Due to recruitment attempts by Calvinist teachers/pastors, non-Calvinists should refuse to sit under their ministries. Calvinists teachers lead new converts into serious doctrinal error. I Cor. 11:3, "For I fear…your minds should be corrupted from the simplicity that is in Christ."

CALVINIST EVANGELISM

IDENTIFYING THE ELECT

Preface

"CALVINIST EVANGELISM" EXPLANATION THEREOF

Who, is to determine who is the "reprobate spirit" non-elect, consigned to burn in hell fire forever? According to Calvinism these cannot be reached, nor won to Christ. Satan, surely as the "great accuser," is quick to influence ministers etc, not to witness to those who "appear" to be reprobate spirits as in the cartoon. Calvinists think it much easier to trust God to "bring the elect into the church as He sees fit. Why go door to door and on streets to win those who would curse and even spit upon us, just work in the realm of the church and let the Holy Spirit "ferret out" the elect (as the Calvinists prefer to do). The false "test" for determining if you are elect or not as Lutzer and other 5 point Calvinists teach simply falls short of being scriptural!

In Lutzer's book "Ten Lies About God" page 147 as follows:

"If you wonder whether you are among the chosen, those whom God foreknew from all eternity, let me encourage you. You can find out whether God granted you grace from all eternity. Simply come to Christ and receive Him by faith; transfer all of your trust to Him for your eternal salvation. He has promised to receive you; your desire to belong to Him is good reason to believe that He has drawn you to Himself (John 1:12).

The problem here is this idea that if you "wonder if you are elect or not supposedly equals the desire to be saved and thus makes you one of the chosen." Naturally it follows that if you "don't wonder if you are one of the elect, then you have no desire to be saved and probably are not of the elect." The simple fact is that there are countless alive today, and even over the past centuries who have/had much aversion to God and salvation thru Christ Jesus, but who eventually did come to Christ and be saved! While Saul of Tarsus was busy murdering Christians, I am sure he had no desire to be "saved" and come to Jesus. Does that mean that he was not one of the elect or does this mean that salvation was "forced" upon him on the road to Damascus? The Lutzer "test" certainly has no scriptural support!

This writer has been a strong soul winner for over 40 years, and has never ever met or known of a single Calvinist who is a strong personal soul winner. Calvinists easily exempt themselves from the burden of door to door, street and personal soul winning on the basis of their fatal-istic doctrine of unconditional election.

CHAPTER ONE
Calvinism the "Other Gospel"

What is the Gospel?
Calvinists claim to hold to the same gospel as we who are opposed to the doctrines of Calvin. In examining the proclamation of what the gospel really consists easily settles this controversy. Notice I Cor. 15:1-4. "Moreover brethren, I declare unto you *the gospel* which I preached unto you, and which also ye have received and wherein ye stand. By which also ye are saved, if ye keep in memory what I preached unto you, unless ye have believed in vain. For I delivered unto you first of all that which I also received how *that Christ died for our sins according to the scriptures. And that he was buried and that he rose again the third day according to the scriptures.*"

Now the battle ground between the two camps is summed up in the one word, "our". To the Calvinists the word "our" refers to only the elect, to the Non-Calvinists it refers to "all" people of all ages Christian and non-Christian. The answer to this conflict is simple. In I Cor. 15 "our" is "faith" speaking of saved people, and that being the "application" of the blood of Christ for Christians. The aspect of "availability" to "all" people of "all" ages is not addressed here but is in many other places such as **1 Jn.2:2, "And He is the propitiation for our sins: and not for ours only but also for the sins of the whole world."** The fact that Paul considers the "gospel" as "good news" could not be "good news" to all people if the elect were sovereignly "pre-saved" in eternity past without their consent! Of course Corinthians was written to Christians, but the "gospel in a nutshell" as Jn. 3:16 is called plainly shows the availability of the gospel was "good news" for "all" of humanity who ever did or will live! (Calvinists believe that the gospel is only "good news" to the saved.) Jn. 3:16. **"For God so loved the world that He gave His only begotten son that whosoever believeth in Him should not perish but have everlasting life."** Now if this verse is only speaking of the elect, (i.e. whosoever being only the elect as the Calvinists falsely teach) then it could not be said that they were ever in any danger of "perishing" having already been "pre-saved/predestined to be saved in eternity past!

Unfortunately there is that element in the church which strongly opposes (and is highly offended at) the revealing/rebuke by authors such as this one, of prominent men who are ensnared by such heretical doctrinal positions as Calvinism, Hardshellism, Armenianism, or other heresies. The simple matter of fact is that **if** anyone has the right to **publicly** preach/teach **anything,** then **anyone** has the right to **publicly** preach/teach for or against those positions and reveal who is preaching it. Hymenaeus and Philetus (see I Tim1:20 and II Tim. 2:17&18) were turned over to Satan due to their propagating false doctrine of the resurrection saying it was already past! False doctrine weakens the church and breeds lawlessness within the ranks of the redeemed! Since when do false teachers have the right to infiltrate and enter the church unchallenged, posing as "prominent Doctors of theology" etc. No man has the right to preach a false system of theology in the church of God! Can God honor a false plan of salvation? Evidently those who refuse to expose/separate from Calvinism think so!

One deadly aspect of Calvinism is that once a pastor etc. embraces its heresies, it has a deadening effect on his love for winning lost souls to Christ, and then gradually produces a cold dead church void of evangelic zeal! John Calvin, according to what this author has read, was not, nor ever was, a soul winner (yes though at times he would minister his theological views to groups of people). While on the run from the persecution of the pope he holed up in a castle in a distant city and being deeply driven into the study of Augustine's works, etc., he eventually wrote his (infamous) "Institutes".

It is this authors opinion, the false doctrine of preordination and election unto salvation by the "sovereignty of God" did appeal to Calvin since for him to go and preach openly in that environment meant certain death at the hands of the Roman Church. If the United States were to issue a death decree upon anyone who preached the gospel, no doubt hundreds of thousands of preachers/ministers would refuse to return to the pulpit. With Calvin, the doctrines of Augustine (sovereign election or unconditional election) would greatly appeal to him relieving him the burden of getting the gospel out at "any cost" due to the fear of Roman persecution! Romans 16:17 plainly commands the church to ..."Mark them which cause divisions and offences contrary to the doctrine which ye have learned and avoid them (i.e. break fellowship with them). So this author sees the need to "identify/mark Calvinism, it's followers, and the T.U.L.I.P."

THE "T.U.L.I.P."

For those unfamiliar with Calvinism's TULIP it is well for this author to give a brief summation of it's meaning.

The "T" stands for Total Depravity.......which according to them simply means that man is totally devoid of any natural/spiritual ability to be anything other than "dead to God", and unable to come to the Lord because of his totally depraved (corrupted by sin) condition. The thought is that being "dead" to God means totally dead spiritually and unable to move toward the Lord in seeking salvation in any sense. (*Dead, as in "Dead in trespasses and sins......" does not mean "unfeeling or insensitive" as the Calvinists teach, but rather means "separated from God by sins and trespasses" in the Biblical sense. Ed.*).

The "U" stands for Unconditional Election, which simply means that the Lord, according to His good pleasure and sovereignty, elects only a certain few of those totally dead souls to eventually be saved, and that that election has nothing to do with foreseen faith, or anything foreseen of anything the "elect one" may do.

The "L" stands for Limited Atonement which says that Jesus was sent to die only for those whom God unconditionally elected to be saved one day, and that while the death of Christ was well "sufficient" for all men, it was only effected and preformed for those elect, thus leaving all others outside the possibility of repentance and conversion to be eternally damned.

The "I" stands for Irresistible Grace meaning that the Holy Spirit is sent to draw only those elected to salvation and that those drawn will ultimately be saved and converted, while all others will be lost to eternal hell and damnation.

The "P" stands for Perseverance of the Saints, which means that those elected and saved will without a doubt remain in a salvation state until death and entrance to heaven. For a full refutation of these points we recommend Dave Hunt's book.... "What Love is This." Calvinism teaches that salvation is not available to all mankind, but that only those few that God especially chooses will enter heaven, while the rest will burn in hell/lake of fire for eternity! Certainly the good news of the gospel according to them is not potentially good news for all mankind.

That this author should find Calvinism to be a serious threat to the stability and welfare of modern day Christianity should come as no surprise to the reader. Calvinism has crept into the most influential churches of our century, and its hideous doctrines have infected some of the most prominent pastors of our churches. Certainly D.L. Moody was no Calvinist....but had a wonderful heart for winning all souls possible. The Calvinist unwittingly believes there are three groups of people categorized on earth to be reckoned with concerning the gospel.

1) There is the "Saved elect group who are regenerated, and ready for heaven.

2) There is the "unsaved but secretly pre-elect" group who need the gospel to be saved.

3) There is the "unsaved group- non-elect due to God's sovereign election" who therefore never can be saved and don't need to be preached to or warned since they are pre-determined to damnation according to the good pleasure of the sovereignty of God.

Now nowhere in scripture is such a picture portrayed! The scripture teaches that there are only the "saved and the unsaved", the "sinner and the saint", the "sheep and the goats", the "wheat and the tares", the "righteous and the unrighteous". Now the scripture is plain that the, saint, the righteous, the sheep, the wheat, the saved ARE TO PREACH TO THE ONLY OTHER GROUP OF PEOPLE BEING IS…..THE SINNER, THE WICKED, THE GOAT, THE TARE, THE UNRIGHTEOUS, THE UNSAVED!! Calvinism thus becomes an escape for the Calvinist from the personal responsibility of winning the lost to Christ (yes they do attempt to win some souls to Christ) and putting all the blame (or credit) on the "sovereignty of God" for the salvation or damnation of souls. Yes, this author understands that Jesus Christ gets ultimate glory for the salvation of lost souls but that does not mean He "forces people to be saved or damned" as Calvinists plainly infer.

The Presbyterian Church U.S.A. in it's "The book of Confessions" follows the Calvinist position closely. Page 125, on "of God's Eternal Decrees"….6.014, … "God from all eternity….did…ordain whatsoever comes to pass…then in 6.020… the rest of mankind (the non-elect) God was pleased …..for the glory of his sovereign power to pass by….and to ordain them to dishonor and wrath for their sin"…*(i.e. the Lord sent them to burn in hell with no chance of ever being saved, because he just sovereignly didn't for some secret reason want to save them. ed.)* Then concerning babies…on page 135, 6.066, "Elect infants dying in infancy are regenerated and saved by Christ through the Spirit….Others, not elected …yet they never truly come to Christ and therefore cannot be saved." 6.067. I ask the reader what kind of God would send infants to a burning hell for eternity?

What babies do they do from pure instinct as their learning process develops. Yes they are born into a sinful world, and will no doubt sin when they come to the age of reason but, nothing of God putting them in hell before they do reach the age of reason! It would be well to notice the heretical work of Calvin....his "Institutes of the Christian Religion" and his perverted view of precious babies and their relationship to God as follows: (After reading the following it may be no wonder if some Calvinistic parents may have a strong tendency **not** to prize and cherish a tiny infant, one which seems to need a never ending "tending to" and one which seems to endlessly cry with continued restlessness and fussing, since in their eyes the baby is a depraved wicked sinner. Also, in strong Calvinist countries, this author wonders if child/infant abuse would be a norm of society there due to Calvin's unscriptural view of a non-elect infants relationship to God).

"INSTITUTES OF THE CHRISTIAN RELIGION"
by John Calvin
Book 4, Ch. 16:17 Subject: Babies
not justified are hated by God.

Quoting Calvin as follows. "In fine, if Christ speaks truly when he declares that he is life, we must necessarily be engrafted into him by whom we are delivered from the bondage of death. But "how?"... they *(ed. "they" being the ones opposed to infants being saved or lost according to election)* ask, are infants regenerated when not possessing a knowledge of either good or evil? We answer that the work of God, though beyond the reach of our capacity, is not therefore null. Moreover, infants who are to be saved (and that some are saved at this age is certain) must without question be previously regenerated by the Lord. For if they bring innate corruption with them from their mothers womb, they must be purified before they can be admitted in the kingdom of God into which shall not enter anything that defiles (Rev. 21:27).

If they are born sinners as David and Paul affirm, they must either remain unaccepted and hated by God or be justified. And why do we ask more when the Judge himself publicly declares that "except a man be born again he cannot see the kingdom of God" John.3:3.

But as to silence this class of objectors, God gave in the case of John the Baptist whom he sanctified from his mother's womb Luke.1:15, a proof of what he might do in others. They gain nothing by the quibble to which they here resort—viz, that this was only once done, and therefore it does not for with follow that the Lord always acts thus with infants. That is not the mode in which we reason. Our only object is to show that they unjustly and malignantly confine the power of God within limits, within which it cannot be confined." Then …Calvin in his "Aphorisms" page 687 in speaking of Baptizing babies…(i.e. elect babies….of course)…..says………. "Forgiveness of sins also belongs to infants, and therefore it is likewise a sign of forgiveness."

Then lastly on the "Decree of God" to consign non elect infants to eternal death *(ed. ..hell)* Book 3, ch.23:7. "I again ask how is it that the fall of Adam involves so many nations with their infant children in eternal death without remedy, unless that it so seemed meet to God? Here the most loquacious tongues must be dumb. The decree I admit is dreadful and yet it is impossible to deny that God foreknew what the end of man was to be before he made him and foreknew because he had so ordained by his decree. Should anyone here inveigh against the prescience of God he does it rashly and inadvisably for why should it be made a charge against the heavenly judge that he was not ignorant of what was to happen? thus if there is any just or plausible complaint it must be directed against predestination."

(ed. To say precious babies are burning and being tormented in hell

fire forever because God supposedly did not elect them is as criminal an offence in this case committed by God, as it would be for someone in this life to do the same to infants by placing them in a burning oven to supposedly "punish" them. Strange we were all horrified recently at the mother who "micro waved" her infant, but many, many Calvinists are given a pass at their belief that God torments babies in hell fire eternally! To endorse true Calvinism is to endorse infanticide and just as well gives abortion a pass since the aborted "elect babies" would naturally go to heaven thus being spared being raised in a sinful world, while the non-elect would go to hell early rather than later thus sparing the world much potential corruption! This alone shows that Calvinism is spiritual insanity, and has no sane rationality).

Remember the precious babies thrown into the burning fiery arms of Moleck in OT. times during idol worship by heathen and sometimes wayward Israel. What an abomination! If Calvinism were true, what sense would it make to torment infants in hell for being what God permitted them to be i.e. potential "sinners". To punish them would be the same as punishing a dog for barking, or a cat meowing or a bird for flying! Augustine, the Roman Catholic Bishop of Hippo (lived 354-430) possibly was the first to introduce the "terrible doctrine of double predestination" as it is often called, and since John Calvin feasted at Augustine's theological table it is no wonder that he picked up this fatal heresy. This author uses the term "fatal heresy" because few if any who digest these false doctrines ever recover theologically.

Augustine taught that while non-baptized children must be damned in a Gehenna of fire, their torments would be light (levissima) compared with the torment of other sinners, and that their condition would be far preferable to non-existence, and so on the

"Calvinism" the Trojan Horse

whole a blessing. In a limbus infantum they would only receive a mitissima damnatio. He also taught that death did not necessarily end probation, as is quite fully shown under "Christ's Descent into Hades." Augustine's idea was reduced to rhyme in the sixteenth century by the Rev. Michael Wigglesworth, of Malden, Mass., who was the Puritan pastor of the church in that place.

A curious fact in the history of the parish is this, (the poem represents God as saying to non-elect infants):

> "You sinners are, and such a share as sinners may expect
> Such you shall have, for I do save none but my own elect
> Yet to compare your sin with theirs, who lived a longer time
> I do confess yours is much less, though every sins a crime
> A crime it is, therefore in bliss you may not hope to dwell
> But unto you I shall allow the easiest room in hell!

(Isn't this wonderful....the Calvinists are able to portray God as having mercy on non-elect infants by His allowing them to forever live on in hell being lightly tormented, rather than to cease their existence!) (interesting it is here that Roman Catholicism has traditionally in the past placed small children in torments of fire in the [*fantacy ed.*] place called "limbo" (oh but God is really good to these children?!). Notice as follows: "A Catholic Book for Children" says: "The fifth dungeon is a red-hot oven in which is a little child. Hear how it screams to come out! see how it turns and twists itself about in the fire! It beats its head against the roof of the oven. It stamps its little feet on the floor of the oven. To this child God was very good. Very likely God saw that this child would get worse and worse, and would never repent, and so it would have to be punished much worse in Hell. So God, in his mercy, called it out of the world in its early childhood." [from Tracts for Spiritual Reading, an officially approved Catholic Children's book. In his Approbation, William Meagher, Vicar-General of Dublin, states *I have carefully read over this Little Volume for Children and have found nothing whatever in it contrary to the doctrines of the Holy Faith; but on the contrary, a great deal to charm, instruct and edify the youthful classes for whose benefit it has been written.*] but then take note coming from the church which claims infallibility....

> **AP Apr. 21 07- Pope Benedict XVI** has reversed centuries of traditional Roman Catholic Teaching on limbo, approving a Vatican report released Friday that says there were "serious" grounds to hope that children who die without being baptized can go to heaven. Theologians said the move was highly significant- both for what it says about Benedicts willingness to buck a long-standing tenant of Catholic belief and for what it means theologically for the Church's view on heaven and original sin- the sin that the faithful believe all children are born with.

The use of such verses of scripture as Ps. 58:3, "The wicked go estranged from the womb they go astray as soon as they be born speaking lies," is used to try to make innocent babies as wicked, lying sinners. But in further reading the context it is evident that these wicked, are "speaking lies" and also have "teeth," see verse 6. Also as well the righteous as in verse10 are seen as rejoicing in the vengeance of God and will be "washing their feet" in the blood of those "wicked," certainly not God taking out wrath and destruction on babies and infants for the righteous to wash their feet in their blood! Common sense dictates that these verses are merely speaking of the fact that the truly wicked have never been converted, and have been in that state of lawlessness from the earliest years of their lives when they were able to learn to speak lies and rebel against God and His laws. One who is not able to discern between right and wrong (a baby or infant or extremely young child) cannot be held accountable for sin. Psalm 51:5, "Behold I was shapen in iniquity and in sin did my mother conceive me," is used to attempt to show babies are born with sin or guilt for sin. The Psalmist here certainly is not saying such, but rather is proclaiming that he was conceived and born into a sinful environment, and that being the case had such sinful influences upon himself (and of course his own choice to do wrong) encouraging his waywardness. To say that all infants are born with the "sin" of Adam imputed to them is not scriptural, rather they do have the "carnal/sin *prone* nature inherited from Adam which will undoubtedly (and without question) be involved in sin when they reach the age of reason and the understanding of God's laws. That "sin prone nature" is innocent until such time, of course unless they are born mentally retarded. Paul in Romans 7:9-12 and James, clearly explain the innocence of a person and their spiritual "life" until their "death" at the age of reason and choice to commit sin by intelligently choosing to disobey God's law. Certainly a Divine put down of Calvinism.

> "For I was alive without the law once: but when the commandment came, sin revived and I died. And the commandment which was ordained to life, I found to be unto death. For sin taking occasion by the commandment, deceived me, and by it slew me. Wherefore the law is holy, and just and good."
>
> James 1:14-15

"For every man *("person" ed.)* is tempted when he is drawn away of his own lust, and enticed. Then when lust hath conceived, it bringeth forth win, and sin when it is finished, bringeth forth death."

David certainly did not wonder if his departed baby was one of the elect or not. (As Calvin would have had he been in the same position!) when the baby died. He clearly said, *"I know he shall not come to me but I shall go to him."*

II Sam. 12:23.

"Calvinism" the Trojan Horse

"CALVINIST PASTOR CONSOLING EXPLANATION THEREOF FOLLOWING

While it "seems" that very few Calvinists today embrace the idea that "non-elect" infants/young children etc go to hell, the irrefutable fact is that those hardcore Calvinists who are faithful to the doctrines of Calvin do embrace that terrible doctrine. (Sadly many Calvinists who do believe this, will not openly admit it, and will hedge the point by saying, "Well we don't know who are elect and who are not, only God knows that," or will say, "Well I cer-tainly do not believe all doctrines that Calvin believed.") Also the irrefutable fact remains that Calvin did embrace that unscriptural hideous doctrine. Therefore those who call them-selves "Calvinists" need to understand that since their leader held that doctrine, they them-selves are guilty by association and name. It must be understood that to endorse Calvin as their leader, they thereby unwittingly endorsing his doctrines. If not then they should not call themselves Calvinists. This cartoon naturally is portraying a hardcore Calvinist pastor attempting to console a grieving couple over the loss of their infant. The cartoon is accurate in exposing Calvin's heartless idea that God consigns non-elect infants to hell fire forever because he for some unknown sovereign reason simply did not elect them to salvation.

THE "WESTMINSTER CONFESSION" PLAINLY TEACHES…

The Presbyterian Church U.S.A. in it's "The book of Confessions" follows the Calvinist position closely. Page 125, on "of God's Eternal Decrees"….6.014, … "God from all eternity….did…ordain whatsoever comes to pass…then in 6.020… the rest of mankind (the non-elect) God was pleased …..for the glory of his sovereign power to pass by….and to ordain them to dishonor and wrath for their sin"…

(i.e. the Lord sent them to burn in hell with no chance of ever being saved, because he just sovereignly didn't for some secret reason want to save them. ed.) Then concerning babies...on page 135, 6.066, "Elect infants dying in infancy are regenerated and saved by Christ through the Spirit....Others, not elected ...yet they never truly come to Christ and therefore cannot be saved." 6.067

CALVIN PLAINLY SAID AND TAUGHT...

Book 4, Ch.16:17 Subject: Babies not justified are hated by God.

Quoting Calvin as follows. "In fine, if Christ speaks truly when he declares that he is life, we must necessarily be engrafted into him by whom we are delivered from the bondage of death. But "how?"... they (ed. "they" being the ones opposed to infants being saved or lost according to election) ask, are infants regenerated when not possessing a knowledge of either good or evil? We answer that the work of God, though beyond the reach of our capacity, is not therefore null. **Moreover, infants who are to be saved. and that some are saved at this age is certain. must without question be previously regenerated by the Lord. For if they bring innate corruption with them from their mothers womb, they must be purified before they can be admitted in the kingdom of God into which shall not enter anything that defiles** (Rev. 21:27).

If they are born sinners as David and Paul affirm, they must either remain unaccepted and hated by God or be justified.

ALSO HE TAUGHT...

Then ...Calvin in his "Aphorisms" page 687 (Calvin's Institutes) in speaking of Baptizing babies...(i.e. elect babies....of course)... says... "Forgiveness of sins also belongs to infants, and therefore it is likewise a sign of forgiveness."

Then lastly on the "Decree of God" to consign non elect infants to eternal death (ed. ..hell) Book 3, ch.23:7. "I again ask how is it that the fall of Adam involves so many nations **with their infant children in eternal death without remedy, unless that it so seemed meet to God?** Here the most loquacious tongues must be dumb. The decree I admit is dreadful and yet it is impossible to deny that God foreknew what the end of man was to be before he made him and foreknew because he had so ordained by his decree. Should anyone here inveigh against the prescience of God he does it rashly and inadvisably for why should it be made a charge against the heavenly judge that he was not ignorant of what was to happen? thus if there is any just or plausible complaint it must be directed against predestination."

Milman observes: *"With shame and horror we hear from Augustine himself that fatal axiom which impiously arrayed cruelty in the garb of Christian charity."* Augustine was the first in the long line of Christian persecutors, and illustrates the character of the theology that swayed him in the wicked spirit that impelled him to advocate the right to persecute Christians who differ from those in power. The dark pages that bear the record of subsequent centuries are a damning witness to the cruel spirit that actuated Christians, and the cruel theology that impelled it.

Augustine "was the first and ablest asserter of the principle which led to Albigensian crusades, Spanish armadas, Netherland's butcheries, St. Bartholomew massacres, the accursed infamies of the

Inquisition, the vile espionage, the hideous bale fires of Seville and Smithfield, the racks, the gibbets, the thumbscrews, the subterranean torture-chambers used by churchly torturers."

Isn't this interesting…"Followers of Calvin a disciple of Augustine."

D. James Kennedy, pastor of Coral Ridge Presbyterian Church, requires his students (students of his "Knox Theological Institute") to subscribe to a Biblical statement of faith AND to the Westminster Confession of Faith….a fully Calvinistic (yea fatalist doctrinal) document. Note here…"The Westminster Confession of Faith" a commentary, authored by Presbyterian scholar G.I. Williamson, Presbyterian and reformed publishing Co. Philadelphia, states their reason for infant baptism. In chapter 26 "Of Baptism", pages 207-216, he states that if an infant is an "elect infant" that at the time of baptism the Holy Spirit regenerates it…planting the seeds of repentance of faith within, so one day it will certainly germinate into the new birth. See also pages 88-95 for further proof of this. (Calvinists today no doubt have picked up this heretical idea of special regeneration unto believing before salvation, and then leading to salvation).

So what happens to the "non-elect infant" who is baptized as well…simple, it is lost and hell bound as "The book of Confessions" so plainly teaches. Sad, what heresy….(Calvinism certainly is "another Gospel). Today, it is my understanding that most Presbyterian scholars lean heavily toward the salvation of all deceased infants, (no doubt warily "eyeing" the potential displeasure of their sleeping parishioners) though that is not the teaching of Calvin nor of the "Book of Confessions" (more on this later) and the "Westminster Confession of Faith.

Calvinism the "Other Gospel"

Erwin Lutzer, the present pastor of the famous Moody Church in Chicago, unfortunately is a strong Calvinist. On Oct. 17, 2000 on his radio broadcast, (as this author was returning from vacation from Indiana), stated that "….I believe that God intended for man to sin". Very consistent with the doctrine of Calvin, i.e. Fatalism. Over the years I have heard Dr. Lutzer often extol the virtues (?) of Calvinist doctrine, convincing me that he unfortunately, is a five point (T.U.L.I.P.) Calvinist. To be fair to Dr. Lutzer this author wrote him asking for his official position on the five points of John Calvin, and as well, I asked him to write a brief answer on why he believed that God intended for man to sin, as well as a few other questions.

He replied as follows: (Jan.16, 2008)

> Rev. Miller-
>
> Although I don't have time to answer all of your questions, I would direct you to my book "Ten Lies About God. The book is currently out of print but probably still available at Amazon.com) There I discuss my view of the fall, God's sovereignty, etc.
>
> *I hold to the five points of Calvinism as long as we understand that Christ's death was sufficient for all but intended to save the elect (ed. emphasis)* I do not however, have a strong desire to see Moody Church become known as one based on Reformed Theology since we believe in believer's baptism, etc.
>
> I believe all children who die will be saved. I hope this helps.
>
> Sincerely, Erwin W. Lutzer
> LAI

"Calvinism" the Trojan Horse

Moody Church was certainly not founded on Calvinism. D. L. Moody was not a Calvinist (see reader note below). Quite ironic that this famous church has a 5 point Calvinist as pastor, clearly a huge departure from it's original founders intent. D. L. Moody, in 1858, began holding Sunday school services for underprivileged children in a rented saloon. Eventually this grew into the great Moody Church and over the years has had a wonderful ministry. In reading the Constitution of the Moody Church, readily available on line, it is clear that according to Article 2, section E, that John 3:16 in its simplicity, (and not being interpreted as the Calvinists do that the "whosoever" and "world" means only the elect) meaning "availability of salvation to all," was the intent of the founders for the church. Since Lutzer is a Calvinist, and sees John Calvin as a "great theologian" (see his book "Ten Lies About God" for quote pg.140), it is evident he would open his pulpit and extend church membership to Calvin and as well teaching privileges in the College were he alive today! (Note: Calvinists make "availability and application" one and the same to be applied only to the elect, while the scriptures teach plainly the two terms apply to all irregardless.)

Now this author asks in the light of the expose of Calvin in "Calvin's Pernicious Theology" in chapter five, how long would Calvin remain a Moody church member in good standing? Also how many Calvinists have now infiltrated the Moody Church? Certainly the church to be true to it's constitution and in the light of all of the afore facts, would be forced to exclude them from fellowship. Article 2, section E of the Moody Constitution reads as follows:

> By Exclusion. It is right, proper, and in harmony with the Scriptures **to exclude from this fellowship any member who holds false and heretical doctrines (Gal.1:8-9),**

or who lives inconsistently with a Christian profession or in violation of the law and/or public morals, or walks disorderly (2Th.3:6-11; 1Co.5:11), **or any member who would disturb the unity and peace of The Moody Church** (Tit.3:10-11; Bylaws Article 2).

The two edged sword here is that if Calvinism be true and scriptural, then Moody church members who believe that any one can be saved, and salvation is available to ALL are the heretics and need to be excluded from church fellowship! Why? Simple, again…. the reason being that they (we) believe the gospel which is, opposite from what the Calvinists believe. Only one can be right! Lutzer in his "Ten Lies About God," (page 145 quoting Charles Alexander) promotes the false premise that God must have decreed, and thus by decree reflected His permission and purpose of sin coming into the world, *(naturally inferring His intention for man to sin. Ed.)* and then redemption unfolding. Lutzer quoting Alexander as follows:

> **"If God were less than omnipotent, or if He allowed evil to develop and multiply itself in His own domain of creation without His prior decree and permission and purpose, then He is not God, and cannot be God. If evil there must be, let us be in the hands of God and not chance, for if evil comes from outside the divine decree, otherwise than by the will of God, then there must be another god beside God."** *(Evidently Alexander doesn't know there certainly is "another god" whose name is "Satan, the god of this world" ed.)*

Reader note: D.L. Moody a Calvinist? Not hardly! "Questions about moody's theology-the five that people ask most often." From "**Love Them In: The Life and**

"Calvinism" the Trojan Horse

Theology of D.L. Moody." By Dr. Stanley N. Gundry, publisher for academic and professional books and general manager of Zondervan Publishing House, Grand Rapids, MI. (Quoting as follows); January 1, 1990 - "Was Moody a Calvinist or an Arminian? Both Calvinist and Arminians cooperated with him in his meetings, although neither camp was entirely comfortable with his views. Moody had been profounldy affected by both the Arminianizing trends of North American Evangelicalism and the more Calvinistic views of British Evangelicals.

Arminians were ill at ease with Moody's "once in grace, always in grace" views, and they were not happy with Moody's statements about election.

But Calvinist felt uncomfortable with Moody's Evangelistic emphasis on human resposibility to believe and the universal provision and offer of salvation. In Moody's words. "I don't try to reconcile God's sovereignty and man's free agency". (End of quote, and also having a five point Calvinist becoming the pastor of perhaps the most famous non-Calvinist Evangelical church in modern church history certainly gives Calvinists a "feather" in their cap and as well gives them much undeserved respect and acceptance among non-Calvinsts).

This false theology which paints God as one who decrees/intends for all men to sin, then decrees for Jesus to come to save only a select few according to His sovereign decree, and then decrees the rest of humanity to burn in hell and the lake of fire for the rest of eternity is totally foreign to the Word of God! There is not one scripture, which teaches that God intended for man to sin, not one! (God was neither the author nor originator of sin!!) That doctrine is merely a doctrine of false reasoning as illustrated by such as Alexander and embraced by Lutzer and other Calvinists. Since Moody Church is evidently being gradually groomed as a Calvinistic Church, it would seem to be only natural to rename it for that doctrinal position, perhaps as "Lutzer Memorial" since eventually, it will no longer reflect the doctrinal position of Dwight L. Moody. (SEE READER NOTE!)
So how can one determine, "if he or she is one of the elect or not" is sure to worry all unsaved who are fed the doctrines of Calvin. Lutzer has that answer in his book "Ten Lies...." Page 147.

"If you wonder whether you are among the chosen, those whom God foreknew from all eternity, let me encourage you. You can find out whether God granted you grace from all eternity. Simply come to Christ and receive Him by faith; transfer all of your trust to Him for your eternal salvation. He has promised to receive you; your desire to belong to Him is good reason to believe that He has drawn you to Himself."

(John 1:12).

The problem here is this idea that if you "wonder if you are elect or not supposedly equals the desire to be saved and thus makes you one of the chosen." Naturally it follows that if you "don't wonder if you are one of the elect, then you have no desire to be saved and probably are not of the elect." (Did Saul of Tarsus wonder if he was one of the elect while killing Christians?) Rather than urge all unsaved we contact to repent and be saved, we are to apply this formula? Nowhere in the Scriptures is such a formula stated, rather the Bible teaches, "God now commands all men everywhere to repent" Acts 17:30. (This formula also teaches that "God granting grace" is really the *["false"- ed.]* doctrine of Unconditional Election!) Away with such fantasies! Speaking of Unconditional Election notice as follows.

The Westminster Short Confession written in about 1640, has a very famous question and answer the Calvinists proudly adhere to which unwittingly is contradictory to unconditional election to say the least. This most famous question contained therein known to a great many Presbyterian children (and piously proclaimed by Calvinists) is the first as follows:

Q. What is the chief end of man?
A. Man's chief end is to glorify God, and to enjoy him forever.

How does this very true statement contradict Calvinism? Notice as follows.

1. When it says "man's" the clear implication is that "all" are included. If unconditional election were true this implication would be a lie.

2. If Calvinism were true then "man's" should be changed to "The elect's" or to "Only those predestined to be saved, and the answer to this "famous" question would then be....

For those elected/ predestined to be saved only, their chief end is to glorify God and to enjoy him forever and the chief end of the non-elect is to be tormented in eternal hell fire forever

Here again, the inconsistency of Calvinistic doctrine is clearly revealed.

Calvinism certainly is "another Gospel." Unfortunately most Calvinists teach there are only three possible points of view…. "Calvinism, Armenianism," or "Unitarianism" which of course is false. There is the other possibility namely that of the **Word of God**… that "any person" is a true candidate of salvation, and once born into the family of God that person is eternally and unconditionally saved forever! Yes certainly, the Word of God does indeed teach predestination, and election, but certainly not the perverted election and predestination of Calvinism!

Sadly, most evangelical/fundamental churches do not understand the serious implications of having a pastor who is a Calvinist, and

Calvinism the "Other Gospel"

ignore that fact if it does come to light since they come to love and respect him during his ministry. A Calvinist will rarely if ever be seen weeping over lost sinners, or making passionate pleas to a congregation, or in personal soul winning for persons to be saved. The reason is simple and evident. The Calvinist believes that any lost souls that are of the non-elect are providentially damned to eternal hell with no hope of salvation anyway, while those elect but not saved yet must and will be saved eventually, in the providence of God so why worry and beg them as well? The bottom line to the Calvinist is that no matter what he does or does not do, the elect will eventually come to Christ and be saved, i.e. fatalism plain and simple. What church needs such a pastor who embraces such false theology and potentially brings deadness in evangelism and personal soul winning with him?

Imagine if you will, the weeping broken hearted parishioner asking the Calvinist pastor to pray with him or her for their lost wayward son or daughter. In that pastors mind, that wayward one's destiny was already determined before the world began by God's sovereign election. How can he be burdened for that lost soul? A burdened soul would denote his belief in the possibility of that soul unnecessarily and possibly going to an eternal hell unless they travail, pray and do all they can to win that lost loved one to Christ! No! Calvinists believe, as already stated that no one is in "danger" of going to hell. The elect are in no danger, they cannot be lost, and the non-elect must go to hell not being elected! They (the non-elect) are not in danger since "in danger" denotes a possibility of damnation or salvation, but the Calvinists teach the non-elect must be damned. Therefore no one is in "danger of being lost" and going to hell according to them. Here is a plain Satanic assault upon the truthfulness of Jesus in warning the wicked about possible impending damnation! To understand this more clearly, think of a man eaten up with cancer and terminally ill. Now what sense would it make to go to the man and tell him, "Sir you are in danger of getting cancer and dying if you do not take the proper precautions." The exact same parallel with Calvinism! Why warn the "non-elect" about the possibility of going to hell eternally and thus give them a false sense of possibility of being saved if Calvinism is true? Certainly therefore, there is no need to "warn" the "elect" since they cannot ever be in "danger of going to hell since they are guaranteed never to be lost! Thus Calvinism brings into disrepute all of the warnings to the unsaved (secretly unknown elect and non-elect) to repent and be saved or suffer eternal damnation. Calvinism unwittingly teaches no one is "in danger" of damnation in hell.

To those who do not see the importance of their pastor **not** being a Calvinist, this author would ask if a church accepts a Calvinist who denies the Biblical plan of salvation as pastor, then why not accept one who denies the deity of Jesus Christ, or denies his bodily resurrection? It's all the same is it not?

Reader note: July 09/09 Lutzer held a special service "honoring" D.L.Moody as a great man! Now what Calvinist believes a non-Calvinist preaches the true gospel when he preaches that "All" can **be** saved as did Moody! Honor Moody indeed!

Here a perfect example of a Calvinist attempting to "ride along on" and be exalted by Moody's well deserved honor. This is more of a funeral eulogy for the Moody church as it becomes a Calvinist institution under Lutzer and his men. (Interesting fact, Sunday 6/10 in his sermon on "Understanding the wrath of God," Lutzer says we need to understand why the wrath of God is against people and nations! Oh!? God's wrath is kindled against those He reprobated to hell???

What's the difference? Or should this author be faulted for exposing serious doctrinal error in the church and for being in favor of a doctrinally pure church? "Heaven forbid we should attempt to have doctrinally pure churches" seems to be the attitude of so many today who seek comfort and consolation in the pew without paying the price to keep the church doctrinally pure by sound church discipline. Compromise is the norm of so many churches, as well as an attitude of "What difference does it really make" by ignorant sleeping parishioners.

One needs only to remember the real problem some of the seven churches of Asia (Rev.3-4), had was to do with false doctrine and spiritual deadness. Ephesus-"Cold dead orthodoxy." Pergamos-"Overtaken by false doctrine." Thyatira- "Teachers teaching deep (depths of Satan) false doctrine," hmmm, sounds like Calvinism. Sardis-"Dead in spirit and works." Laodicea-"Wealthy but spiritually/doctrinally blind." Notice also the threat of severe punishment, which our Savior leveled at those offending churches unless they repent! Calvinism can only bring spiritual deadness and judgment to the church. Forget revival in such a church.

Break fellowship with Calvinists since they preach another plan of salvation? That question is self-evident. Absolutely! (See II Thess. 3:6,14,15 and Rom. 16:17). Allowing Calvinism to infiltrate and exist in our fundamental churches is truly "sleeping with the enemy within."

TEN REASONS FOR BREAKING FELLOWSHIP WITH CALVINISTS

1. To continue fellowshipping with Calvinists is to endorse them as worthy of doctrinal fellowship which they are not.

2. To continue fellowshipping with Calvinists is to set a bad example to those entrusted to our ministry, and well could stumble them into doctrinal error.

"Calvinism" the Trojan Horse

3. To continue fellowshipping with Calvinists is to make them think we are endorsing their ministries and consider them our equals in the ministry, which they are not..

4. To continue fellowshipping with Calvinists is to violate plain scriptural command to "Mark them and avoid them which cause divisions in the church." Romans 16:17.

5. To continue fellowshipping with Calvinists opens our pulpits to them, when in fact they generally refuse to allow us in theirs.

6. To continue fellowshipping with Calvinists shows a refusal on our part to rebuke them for serious doctrinal error.

7. To continue fellowshipping with Calvinists could possibly weaken us in our doctrinal positions by exposure to their heresies.

8. To continue fellowshipping with Calvinists quenches and grieves the working of the Holy Spirit in and through us and can set us aside from spiritual blessings, and as well prevent revival.

9. To continue fellowshipping with Calvinists allows that heresy to go unchallenged and thus flourish and grow.

10. To continue fellowshipping with Calvinists shows a weakness and willingness on our part to compromise with false doctrine.

It must be remembered that reformed theology came out of the Reformation and in particular the theology of John Calvin (1509-1564), although its roots go back to Augustine (345-430), it was formulated by the Puritans, especially in the Westminster confession of faith (1646). This Confession is the enduring fruit of the solemn Assembly of some 100 leading Puritan divines, convened at Westminster Abbey in London from July 1, 1643 through to Feb.1649. Other reformed confessions: Belgic (1580), Baptist (1689), 39 Articles of the Church of England - Anglican and Episcopal (1571, 1662, 1801) ed.)

THE GOD OF CALVINISM DECREEING/ CAUSING MAN TO SIN

"..we say that God once established by his eternal and unchangeable plan those whom he long before determined once for all to receive into salvation, and those whom, on the other hand, he would devote to destruction. ...he has barred the door of life to those whom he has given over to damnation." Calvin's institutes, book 3, Ch 21, s. 7

"Again I ask: whence does it happen that Adam's fall irremediably involved so many peoples, together with their infant offspring, in eternal death unless because it so pleased God? ... The decree is dreadful indeed, I confess. Yet no one can deny that God foreknew what end man was to have before he created him, and consequently foreknew because he so ordained by his decree...And it ought not to seem absurd for me to say that God not only foresaw the fall of the first man, and in him the ruin of his descendants, but also meted it out in accordance with his own decision…" Bk 3, Ch 23, s. 7

"There can be no election without its opposite, reprobation." (Institutes, Book 3, Chapter 23)

CALVINISM AND THE WHEAT AND TARES

To show how far out the doctrines of Calvinism are, one needs only to examine the parable of the wheat and the tares and it's parallel to the gospel to see how anti-Biblical those doctrines are. Read as follows:

Matthew 13:24-30 & 37-43

Another parable put he forth unto them saying. The kingdom of heaven is likened unto a man which sowed good seed in his field. But while men slept, his enemy came and sowed tares among the wheat and went his way. But when the blade was sprung up, and brought forth fruit, then appeared the tares also. So the servants of the householder came and said unto him, Sir didst not thou sow good seed in thy field? From whence then hath it tares? He said unto them, An enemy hath doe this. The servants said unto him. Wilt thou then that we go and gather them up? But he said, Nay lest while ye gather up the tares, ye root up also the wheat with them. Let both grow together until the harvest. I will say to the reapers, Gather ye together first the tares and bind them in bundles to burn them: but gather the wheat unto my barn. (vs, 37-43 following). He answered and said unto them, He that sowed the good seed is the Son of man. The field is the world, the good seed are the children of the kingdom but the tares are the children of the wicked one. The enemy that sowed them is the devil: the harvest is the end of the world and the reapers are the angels. As therefore the tares are gathered and burned in the fire, so shall it be in the end of this world. The Son of man shall send forth his angels and they shall gather out of his kingdom all things that offend and them which do iniquity: And shall cast them into a furnace of fire: there shall be wailing and gnashing of teeth. Then shall the righteous shine forth as the sun in the kingdom of their Father. Who hath ears to hear let him hear.

Reader note: Recently Lutzer stated, "The lost sinner's only hope to stay out of hell, is to turn to Jesus for salvation." That sounds good but according to Calvinism, the only hope for a lost sinner to stay out of hell is to hope that God sovereignly elected him to salvation, so outside of that hope according to Calvin, there can be no other hope. Therefore for the Calvinist to use the "only hope is to turn to Jesus" as an incentive for the sinner to repent is insincere and as well is a false/deceitful Calvinistic prompt to act as a non-Calvinist in his evangelistic attempt to win the lost. He wants to sound like a "non-Calvinist" but in so doing he betrays his hypocrisy. This can easily be seen by the simple fact that the Calvinist wouldn't dare preach, "Your only hope for salvation is whether or not God elected you," which is what Calvinism really stands for. The bottom line for the Calvinist in the salvation of lost sinners is not whether or not we can win them to Christ, but rather whether or not they are of the elect! The Calvinist is not therefore preaching what he really and truly believes in such a case.

NOW IF CALVINISM BE TRUE ARE WE TO BELIEVE THE FOLLOWING?

1. That Jesus sowed good seed/gospel seed into the world, and at the same time He commissioned/ordained/sent Satan to sow bad seed among the good? According to Calvinism (and the Westminster Confession *["of heresy"* ed.), God ordaining/decreeing all things that take place in the world in all ages then becomes the originator/author/enabler of Satan's working to send people to burn in everlasting torment. God intended this?

2. That then man has no true bottom line in determining his eternal destiny but rather is "set up" to fall by the hand of the Almighty. God intended this?

3. That God naturally being the first "cause" of all in His creation was the cause of the enemy Satan, to go throughout the world bringing evil and causing men to crucify Jesus and reject the plan of salvation. God intended this?

4. That God as creator of all there is, created Lucifer and all the angels, His intention being for Lucifer to rise up with pride, sin and shame, bringing down a third of the angels with him. Calvinism teaches, as already shown, that God "intended" for man to sin, so if that is the case then God also intended for Satan and his angels to sin as well! God intended this?

5. That considering all of the above, God was in reality the author and originator of sin, and thus the originating power behind all of the evil, depravity, shame and disgrace in the world since the dawn of creation? God intended this?

6. That God, as all must admit, cannot sin nor be charged with sin or unrighteousness, so in reality we must not call sin evil or wrong since God authored it and intended for Satan and man to sin. Are we to believe this?

7. That any person who believes the above has any credibility, scriptural right or calling to be a pastor, missionary, evangelist, teacher or whatever in the church of God? God intends that?

8. Are we to believe that God and Satan have the same purpose for all men? If God indeed intended for man

to sin, then He had collusion with Satan in bringing that about. Are we to believe this?

Now it stands to reason, if all of the above be true, as Calvinism teaches (wittingly or unwittingly) then there can be no such thing as sin, right, wrong, good or evil since God authored it all! This author's hat is off for Calvinism showing it's own untenable, preposterous anti-Biblical doctrines. Away with such foolishness. Below as already stated and quoted from Calvin we quote again, and then use the same convoluted logic to insert Satan's name in his quote following.

CALVIN'S GOD INTENDED FOR MAN TO SIN

"The first man fell because the Lord deemed it meet that he should:"…….. "Nor ought it to seem absurd when I say, that God not only foresaw the fall of the first man, and in him the ruin of his posterity; but also at his own pleasure arranged it." by John Calvin.

Calvin's Institutes Chapter 23, 3:7&8.

CALVIN'S GOD INTENDED FOR LUCIFER TO SIN AND HE WOULD SAY…

"The first angel Lucifer and one third of the other angels fell because the Lord deemed it meet that they should: …Nor ought it seem absurd when I say, that God not only foresaw the fall of Satan and his angels and their pending eternal damnation; but also at his own pleasure arranged it." *(Calvin may not have said this, but he had to have believed it! Ed.)* It is safe to say Calvin believed that God intended for Lucifer and man to sin and fall!

SATAN NOT THE RIVAL OR ADVERSARY OF GOD?

In the November 2010 issue of "Midnight Call" which is a strong fundamentalist pre-trib rapture magazine edited by Arno Froese, based in Columbia, S.C. the following shocking and defamatory declaration was made about God. (Dr. Ron J. Bigalke author).

> "As Martin Luther said **in agreement with Scripture**, "Satan is God's devil;" he is not a rival but God just uses him to accomplish His purposes. The church does not have that power. According to Jude 9, dispute with the devil must be on the basis of the Lord's rebuke. Even Michael the archangel recognized that only God could oppose Satan." (Article page 27, "Second Thessalonians 2 And The Rapture.")

1. So first he says that "Satan is God's devil." The defamatory here is that God supposedly "owns" Satan!? Now if God "owns" Satan, then He as well "owns" Satan's actions as well, making Himself fully culpable and responsible for all sin and depravity issuing from Satan's activities, and as well makes Himself (God) the author of sin. This writer has little doubt a Calvinist may be speaking here. No! God does not "own" Satan, and Satan is clearly referred to as the great Adversary of God and His people (II Pet. 5:8) and as well is (Jn. 8:44) "…a liar and the father of it." Bigalke also says "…in agreement with Scripture," so we must ask "What Scripture?" Truly the stench of Calvinism rises here since John Calvin, (as we have earlier pointed

out), clearly stated that "...God intended for man to sin." Now if God "intended" for man to sin then certainly He intended for Satan to sin/fall as well.

2. Then further he says, "...he is not a rival *(of God. ed).*" Now does not this contradict the account of the fall of Lucifer from his first estate in Isaiah 14:12-15 where he was lifted up with pride and wanted to exalt himself above the stars to be equal with God, and thus was cast from heaven? Clearly he became a "rival" of God and was thrown from heaven because of it. Did not Satan rival God in attempting to cause Jesus to bow down before him in the wilderness temptation to worship at his feet? Did not Jesus rebuke him and tell him that "...it is written that thou shalt worship the Lord thy God." Lk. 4:6-8.

3. The accusation by Bigalke that "...God just uses him (Satan) to accomplish His purposes..." contradicts the Biblical teaching that the Holy Spirit is really the one who (Jn.16:8) "... reproves *(convicts)* the world of sin, righteousness and judgment." Pray tell, what noble, honorable, scriptural, righteous, Godly deeds and tasks is Satan sent forth from the hand of God to perform for mankind? The answer is absolutely none! (We should ask Bigalke if the Church should employ the mafia to carry out its plans and purposes!) Satan can do nothing but evil, and any seeming good he may perform, he always performs with a goal in the end of only evil and shame to humanity. See Eph. 2:2.

4. He further falsely states that "...the church does not have the power...to accomplish His purposes..." Oh? Well Jesus thought so. He plainly told the early church that they would be endued with power from on high when the Holy Spirit came upon them on the Day of Pentecost (Acts 1:8). As well Paul plainly told the church to (James 4:7), "...resist the Devil and he will flee from you." With this aberrant theology Bigalke's church probably doesn't have the power for overcoming Satan.

Calvinism the "Other Gospel"

"CALVIN'S GOD PLANNING THE FALL OF MAN" EXPLANATION THEREOF FOLLOWING

No doubt, there are many reading these revelations about Calvin and his theology for the first time, so it is no surprise if many are angered and in ignorance deny that he taught such. One has but to examine his "Institutes of Theology" however, to find differently. Notice as follows:

"The first man fell because the Lord deemed it meet that he should:"........ "Nor ought it to seem absurd when I say, that God not only foresaw the fall of the first man, and in him the ruin of his posterity; but also at his own pleasure arranged it." by John Calvin.

Calvin's Institutes Chapter 23, 3:7& 8.

Now it only stands to reason that if Calvin believed God intended for man to sin and fall, then no doubt he believed the same about the fall of Satan. It is easy to surmise the statement he would make concerning such were he alive today! Since Calvin believed that God caused man to sin and fall, then no doubt he would have stated as follows about the fall of Lucifer:

"The first angel Lucifer and one third of the other angels fell because the Lord deemed it meet that they should: ......Nor ought it seem absurd when I say, that God not only foresaw the fall of Satan and his angels and their pending eternal damnation; but also at his own pleasure arranged it."

Thus, Calvin had to have believed that God intended for Lucifer and man to sin and fall!

CALVIN'S GOD INTENDED FOR LUCIFER TO SIN MAKING GOD THE AUTHOR OF SIN !!

CALVINISTS AND EPHESIANS 1:11

"In whom also we have obtained an inheritance, being predestinated according to the purpose of him who worketh all things after the counsel of His own will"

Calvinists claim that this verse is perhaps the landmark authority for saying that God "ordains" everything that happens. Following is an exchange between a follower of Calvin and a non-Calvinist Pastor friend.

Pastor J.L.

This theological position *(Calvinism-ed)* makes God a monster. It makes Him responsible for sin, the fall of man, the rebellion of Lucifer and the angels, and every evil and horrible thing that demonized people do.

Jared (Calvinist)

Ephesians 1:11 directly contradicts the idea that God does not ordain everything that happens. In him we have obtained an inheritance, having been predestined according to the purpose of him who works all things according to the counsel of his will, This verse says that God works all things according to the counsel of His will. One way to make sense of this is to talk about two wills in God, His perfect or revealed will and His permissive or hidden will. If God's will cannot be thwarted and He works all things according to the counsel of His will, then how can we say that He doesn't ordain everything that happens?

Does God allow everything that happens? Most Christians would say yes.

Does God have a purpose for everything that He allows to happen? I believe He does, otherwise children that are born out of wedlock that weren't planned would be accidents in every sense of the word, and most people wouldn't want to say that.If God allows everything that happens to happen, and He has a purpose for allowing everything that happens, then it's not a very big leap to move from there to say that He ordains everything that happens.

Now, to be sure, God is not the author of sin. He doesn't force people to sin. But, He does providentially orchestrate circumstances to ensure that His will is never thwarted. God never violates our freewill, but He works things out in such a way so as to preserve our freewill and His total sovereignty. God gets what He wants and we get what we want.

Pastor J.L. Response to Jared ...
Dear brother, Eph 1:11 DOES NOT say that God ordains everything that happens.

That is a misconception and erroneous interpretation. It is a brittle stretch to say this verse supports that supposition that is the heart and core of reformed theology. The Bible states that God is light, and in Him THERE IS NO DARKNESS AT ALL. It is impossible for a holy and righteous God to commit moral evil. Therefore God cannot ordain the sinful actions of wicked people. Any theology that makes God responsible for sin, evil, immorality, wickedness is perverted theology. The church is elected of God, and God has predestined her to a wonderful inheritance. God has a plan and a purpose for the Church. He is working to bring His will to pass. However, He must have the cooperation of those within the Church in order for the destiny of the Church to be fulfilled.

As long as part of the Church of God delays and disobeys God the will of God is hindered.

According to the Bible, God's will is sometimes thwarted. God's will was for Adam and Eve to refrain from eating the forbidden fruit. They disobeyed Him. God's will was that the Children of Israel possess the land of inheritance, Canaan land. Moses sent spies into the land on a recon mission. They returned saying that it was too much for them, that they could not do what God commanded them to do. God called their response an "evil report" and spoke judgment on them, they would die in the wilderness. Their disobedience and sin thwarted the will of God for them. They wandered in the wilderness for 40 years until that generation died off. Only Joshua and Caleb entered into their inheritance. God's will was that He Himself be King over the nation of Israel. They demanded a king like the nations around them. They rejected God's revealed will and purpose and did what they wanted to do in opposition to God's will. People "limited" the God of Israel. They hindered the will of God from being done.

God commands all men everywhere to repent. That is a revelation of His will, yet all men do not repent. Therefore, God's will is thwarted. Does God allow everything that happens? Yes. But that is an entirely different thing than to say that He commissions or ordains everything. God will allow you to do something stupid, like go out and lay down in the middle of a busy highway, but He doesn't ordain you to do it. God will allow you to rob a bank, or break into a house, but He doesn't commission you to steal, He actually commands you to not steal. God will allow a Church member to not pay his tithes, but calls for His people to bring their tithes and offerings unto Him. They do not obey God's will.

Does God have a purpose in everything that happens? CERTAINLY NOT!!! God is NOT behind everything that happens. Many things in the Bible are called the work of the Devil.

"Calvinism" the Trojan Horse

Why do Calvinists ignore what God commands regarding the Devil? The Bible says to resist the Devil, to cast him out, to stand against him, to oppose him and his works, ... it NEVER tells us to lay down and let the Devil run all over us. To say that God ordains everything that happens means that He has to be the author of sin.

Sin happens ...but God doesn't manufacture it.

SO WHERE DID SIN ORIGINATE?

So we see Calvinism's inference that God is the author of sin, since naturally He is the first cause and Calvin clearly taught that God intended for man and Satan to sin and fall. This assertion as well makes God and Satan in collusion to bring the entire human race into sin, debauchery, and everlasting damnation disgrace and shame! Thus, Calvinism is clearly blasphemy against God and His Christ. Who can possibly deny such? To answer the above question is simple. When God created the angels and man, He had three choices, and only three. First to create them above Himself (making Himself subject to His creation which of course is impossible), equal to Himself (which of course would have made two separate Deities), or lesser than Himself, and if lesser than Himself then of course subject to His will and rule (the only possibility). God gave man and the angels' two things which were perfect in their creation. The first was to give them free will, and second to give them perfect warning not to violate His commands. Man and angel were created perfectly educated, so whatever choice they made, to obey or to disobey God's will was perfectly theirs without God interjecting His will. So, God had no intention for man to sin, but to only love him, and as well be the recipient of his love and worship in return. God wanted no man to be forced to love and worship Him, only freely so. Forced worship and love is only mechanical and does not interest God. God never "intended" for man (or the angels) to sin, they did so of their own free will and volition.

Reader note: A fatal weakness of Calvinism is that it teaches man does not have a free will, but rather his will is enslaved to always choose wrong and evil, making it God's duty to force man to what HE desires. Thus forced salvation and forced damnation. The simple fact is however that the scriptures abound with commands of the Lord to both sinner and saint to repent, and choose to do that which is right! This fact alone proves that God expects man to act freely of his own volition to obey and then brings judgment on those who fail to do so! Are we to believe that God planned and arranged for man to have no free will, and then punish him when he is forced thereby to sin and do evil? Calvinists think so!

CHAPTER TWO
Fairly Proposing Calvinism

This author is convinced that the stench of Calvinism no doubt reaches to heavens shores. Imagine if the Calvinist/Reformed Presbyterian/Baptist (etc.) churches saturated with this heresy, were to give out the below flyer at the doors of their worship services, made especially for the "unsaved" who may wander into their services. It would only be fair for these unsaved/unregenerate persons to know the true doctrine of the services they are about to attend. Following is the sample flyer they should give out to these "Potential Saints".

WELCOME YE SINNERS TO OUR SERVICES!

> We Welcome All unsaved unregenerate potential elect persons to our services! We stand proudly upon the doctrines of John Calvin

It is only fair to inform you who are unregenerate, as to your potential standing in God through faith in Christ, and also of the peril you face according to our belief in the sovereignty of Almighty God in election! Please be aware of the following scriptural Calvinistic facts:

"Calvinism" the Trojan Horse

1. You may not be one of the elect that God chose from before the foundation of the world to be saved.

2. You cannot choose Christ for your salvation unless you are one of God's elect from eternity past.

3. God **does not** elect you to salvation due to YOUR choice of Christ (foreseen) or any merit in you foreseen by the omniscience of God. God sovereignly chooses those HE and HE alone wants to be saved from eternal hell.

4. You will go to hell for eternity unless _God_ has elected you to be saved. Only time will tell.

5. You can have no interest or desire to be saved unless you are one of God's elect. If you have no interest in being saved you are not one of God's elect (however time could show differently) and you will probably suffer in the lake of fire for all of eternity because God did not elect you to salvation and make you repent, believe and be saved.

6. Please do not try to understand how God elects persons to be saved, we don't even know except to say it is according to his Sovereignty, He is sovereign and does what He wants, the way He wants, and when He wants.

7. If you wind up in Hell and later the Lake of Fire, you deserve it because you are a hopeless sinner outside of the grace and the scope of God's election, and <u>cannot</u> be saved unless He sovereignly elects you.

8. Do not charge God as being unfair if you go to Hell forever since God is perfect and cannot be charged with sin!

9. We are not like the non-reformed non-Calvinistic churches. We unlike they, will not beg, cajole, plead or coax you to be saved in any manner whatsoever, since God's Holy Spirit alone can draw you to be saved. Please feel free therefore to attend our services in the hopes of discovering whether or not you are one of God's elect.

10. If, after a time of attending our services you do not discover you are one of God's elect, feel free to stay and rejoice with us who are saved! Rejoice with us that God has elected us, while we probably will somehow feel badly that you are not one of God's elect.

11. Feel free to financially support our church and help us in our enjoyment of God, His salvation and election of us while we sincerely hope God has elected you also! We will have absolutely no persuasive altar calls, since you cannot even come to God unless you are called and elected. **We do not believe that everyone can be saved!** Attend as long as you like.

12. If you are not one of God's elect, make certain to enjoy the life you have to the fullest now and have all of the pleasures there, since you are a Hell deserving sinner who is depraved spiritually and not able to come to Christ. Live for all the pleasures of time you can afford….eternity in hell is a long time!

13. Lastly (as your potential new pastor) if one of your smaller children should perish, it is only fair to tell you that due to our belief in "sovereign election or unconditional election" we cannot assure you that the deceased went to heaven (perhaps the little one was not sovereignly elected). We will morn with you and do all in our power to comfort you! Thank you for coming.

Sincerely hoping you and
your loved ones are of the elect.
Sincerely Pastor I.M. Elect. d.d. th.g.

Fairly Proposing Calvinism

THE CALVINIST JESUS PREACHING

A FALSE WARNING
EXPLANATION THEREOF

The Calvinists do indeed tamper with the Biblical plan of salvation by falsely claiming that not all can be saved, but that we are still called to preach the gospel to all the world i.e. to every creature.

Quoting from this booklet on page 5 as follows:
How anyone would dare tamper with the sacred precious plan of salvation, designed and executed by Almighty God! Calvinism certainly does indeed tamper with the plan of salvation, from being that Jesus died for all men, and is the Savior of all men especially of those that believe (1Tim.4:10) and that anyone can be saved, to only a select few are sovereignly elected and can be saved while the rest of the majority are "passed over" in God's secret election and are therefore consigned to burn in hell for eternity!

No Calvinist will deny that we are commanded to preach to all. Such being the case, then if that were true (that not all can be saved), then when one preaches the warnings of Jesus about the possibility of going to hell, that terrible place of suffering, He would be lying and preaching falsely to everyone! Further quoting from this booklet, page 26 following:

Salvation of the elect is pre-determined according to Calvinism so no unsaved person is in danger of going to hell if he or she is one of the elect! On the same token, according to Calvinism, a "non-elect unsaved person" is "not in danger" of going to hell since he has no hope of salvation anyway. "In danger of going to hell" implies that he could possibly be saved and in danger of not being saved when, in reality (according to Calvinism), he is pre-ordained to be damned with no hope of salvation!

Thus that this cartoon fairly portrays the Calvinist Jesus is irrefutable. The god of Calvinism is not the God of the Bible.

A CALVINIST CAN NEVER HONESTLY PREACH TO A CONGREGATION AS FOLLOWS

"If any of you are here today and are not saved, you can certainly receive Jesus Christ and become a born again child of God. If you are not saved you are in danger of dying in your sins and going to a Godless hell. All here today who are unsaved, are invited by the Lord to come forward to receive Christ and be saved.

THE REASON AS FOLLOWS

1. Calvinists say many unsaved in a congregation cannot be saved or wooed to Christ because they are not one of the elect. (Calvinists hide behind the. "Just preach to all since no one knows for sure just who of the unsaved are elect or not".)

2. Calvinists do not believe that ANY unsaved are in danger of going to hell (being "in danger" implies the possibility of someone being lost)! Reason being (using Calvinists logic): Those elect but unsaved yet, have no danger since they are elect and thus have no danger of being lost since they are pre-ordained to be saved, and the non-elect unsaved are pre-ordained to be damned with no chance of salvation, so without a chance to be saved they can be "in no danger or in no hope of salvation anyway"…their fate is already set.

"Calvinism" the Trojan Horse

They are to burn in eternal hell fire under the wrath of Almighty God because He simply for some supposed secret reason decided not to elect them to salvation.

WHAT BLASPHEMY AND INSULT TO THE CROSS OF JESUS AND HIS OFFER OF SALVATION TO "WHOSOEVER WILL, LET HIM COME DRINK OF THE WATER OF LIFE!" (Yes this author is well aware the Calvinists teach the infamous heresy that the "whosoever will" is referring only to those elected but not saved yet). Summing it up:

Salvation of the elect is pre-determined according to Calvinism so no unsaved person is in danger of going to hell if he or she is one of the elect! On the same token, according to Calvinism, a "non-elect unsaved person" is "not in danger" of going to hell since he has no hope of salvation anyway. "In danger of going to hell" implies that he could possibly be saved and in danger of not being saved when, in reality (according to Calvinism), he is pre-ordained to be damned with no hope of salvation! So Calvinism infers Jesus lied about the dangers of hell.

The late Dr. Oliver B. Greene, one to this last centuries greatest radio/author/tent revivalists ever, has a very good tract booklet on "Elected to Heaven or Hell", (order from "the Gospel Hour, box 2024, Greenville, S.C. 29602). He points out that Calvinism must teach that all non elect are **not** lost. He states in essence that the Calvinists say Jesus came only to die for, and save only the elect. He wisely points out that if that is true, then according to Lk.19:10 (which says that "The Son of man came to seek and save that which is lost,") only the elect, for whom Christ supposedly only came to save, are lost! Now I must add, if that is true, then the doctrine of "universal salvation" must be true since if only the elect are lost (promised

Fairly Proposing Calvinism

eventually to be saved), then the non-elect are safe or saved, meaning all would be saved one day! Now what Calvinist believes in universal salvation? Greene also points out that to "preach the gospel to every creature" would make God a criminal for offering salvation to the non elect, knowing that they could not be saved if Calvinism were true. Thank God it is not true!

Dr. Greene further points out…"Now would you accuse God of having me warn a man, who could not be saved, because he was not included in the elect?" What cruelty….to believe God would offer an ice cold drink to a man dying of thirst, knowing that the man was unable to drink due to some physical condition! So does the Lord have us offer salvation to all non-elect and elect unsaved sinners knowing that he has preordained some to eternal hell fire? The scriptures certainly do not teach that! Whosoever will let him come and drink of the water of life, as the scriptures plainly say.

The Calvinists must believe that the rich man in hell was there because he was not elected by the sovereignty of God and that his five brothers were coming to hell also for the same reason. No! Abraham told him that they needed to take heed to "Moses and the prophets", not that election was the determining factor! The word "gospel" means "good news." Calvinism unwittingly teaches that the gospel <u>does not</u> bring the good news of salvation to all men! They teach "limited atonement", which teaches the gospel is good news only to the elect, so that being the case means the "non-elect" have no hope of access to free salvation and the gospel is not "good news" to them!

(What idiocy, what blasphemous dribble)! Calvinists are not burdened to preach the gospel to "every creature" as Jesus commanded since they do not believe that…

(1)   God wants to save every person.

"Calvinism" the Trojan Horse

(2) All could potentially be saved, since not all were or are of the elect. What an insult to God, Calvinists saying that Jesus does not want to save all people, but we should preach to all people to ferret out the elect, thus leaving the non-elect to be damned.

(3) Anyone is in danger of going to hell as stated above.

Lastly I always hear the Calvinists proudly boast of "Sinners in the Hands of an Angry God" by Jonathan Edwards, a very famous sermon preached by one of their own "reformed" ministers, Presbyterian I believe. That this sermon did have a wonderful and powerful impact on its hearers is of no doubt, and I after reading it, must concur that it is indeed a wonderful sermon. BUT... The fact is it theologically contradicted Edwards Calvinist positions....making it a sermon Edwards could not have really believed according to his theological position but he preached it anyway (now is that not blatant hypocrisy). As stated above, how could "sinners be in the hands of an angry God" something like "walking on rotting rags over hell and ready to fall thru at any moment"...(read his sermon) if the doctrine of "unconditional election" which he believed were true? Edwards certainly held the doctrine of unconditional election, but unwittingly contradicts it by preaching that all lost sinners need to repent else face eternal damnation. Note as follows:

> **Jonathan Edwards said:** "The world will probably be converted into a great lake or liquid globe of fire, in which the wicked shall be overwhelmed, which will always be in tempest, in which they shall be tossed to and fro, having no rest day or night, vast waves and billows of fire continually

rolling over their heads, of which they shall forever be full of a quick sense within and without; their heads, their eyes, their tongues, their hands, their feet, their loins and their vitals, shall forever be full of a flowing, melting fire, fierce enough to melt the very rocks and elements; and, also, they shall eternally be full of the most quick and lively sense to feel the torments; not for one minute, not for one day, not for one age, not for two ages, not for a hundred ages, nor for ten thousand millions of ages, one after another, but forever and ever, without any end at all, and never to be delivered."

According to Calvinists, NO SINNER is in danger of dropping into hell. All of humanity is either elect to be saved before birth, or pre-elect to be damned, with no choice of their own, but only according to the "sovereign pleasure of God's will and purpose were they so chosen! Dr. Oliver Greene points out, "I suppose those five boys died in their sins and went to hell like their rich brother who prayed for them not to come. But if they are there, it is because they did not hear the Word of God given to Moses and the prophets, not because they were elected to go to hell!"

During the revivals, Edwards of the 1700's and his Calvinist/Reformed theology was evidenced with a lack of understanding of properly winning lost souls to Christ, souls under conviction of sin. In the Biography...."Jonathan Edwards...A New Biography" by Iain H. Murray, pub. By The Banner of Truth, 621 Carlisle, Pa., Edwards told of several groups of young people who were deeply under conviction of sin, after some services they were deeply affected by (at his first encounter with them). Rather than gather these young people

"Calvinism" the Trojan Horse

around himself and lead them to Christ, he merely stood by and observed their actions. Several years later he came across some of these same persons, and he noticed sadly that they had no more conviction or interest in "religion"!!

So sad indeed...the fatalistic Calvinist theology so mired his thinking that rather than lead them to saving faith in Christ he simply "left them to the sovereignty of Almighty God!" No doubt, thanks to Calvinism, they probably went to hell. Another point on page128 tells it plainly starting in line five......... "Edwards and his brethren consequently denied that 'believe on the Lord Jesus Christ' was the one message to be addressed to the unconverted. Certainly that command presents the one term of salvation, and as such, it is to be made known to all, but something else is first needed to make the command relevant...." What was that? No doubt they believed they needed the Holy Spirit to "regenerate them" which would eventually lead to their repentance and subsequent salvation!, i.e.: they needed the full influence of Calvinistic theology. Edwards sermon, though very scriptural indeed would, in this authors opinion, be tantamount to praising a Watchtower minister whom rejects the doctrine of the Deity of Christ, for preaching that Jesus was indeed Jehovah come in the flesh to a group of non-religious type persons.

(It is noteworthy that he preached an anti-Calvinist type sermon to see the wonderful revival fires, which the church experienced under his ministry!)

Dr. Erwin Lutzer on his broadcast today Jan.6, 2008, in noting the "great awakening", wrongly attributed the great revivals to "**God deciding**" to do something wonderful from time to time and bring revival as He so desired. Wrong, wrong! Revivals do not depend upon "God" but rather God blesses the preaching of Biblical truths which can bring revival if and when people repent and respond. Calvinism certainly does not do that! Dr. Lutzer has overlooked 2 Chronicles 7:14 "If my people, which are called by my name, shall humble themselves and pray and turn from their wicked ways, then will I hear from heaven and will forgive their sins and heal their land'.

The simple truth, in reality, was that the churches Edwards fellowshipped with were Calvinistic/Fatalistic dead and stagnating ministries making parishioners "wait to see if they were of the elect or not". The sermons Edwards preached in the "Great Awakening Period" were decidedly NOT reformed Calvinistic/fatalistic messages, but rather called upon all to exercise their free will to repent and be saved Yes a true breath of fresh air! Certainly the doctrines of John Calvin never have, nor ever will produce revival fires!.) What hypocrisy! Should a preacher get credit for preaching something as true when he theologically rejects it? I certainly do not think so!

While most today who follow John Calvin's system of theology praise and eulogize him, it is this authors opinion that he was NOT a regenerate man (he attempting to ascend on high to be like the Almighty with a new gospel) but a wolf in sheep's clothing. For any man to change the glorious gospel of Jesus Christ, that Jesus died for, **and offers free salvation to all men everywhere**, to a false gospel of fatalism, forced salvation and forced damnation, (and as well as "infants and small children if not elect in the flames of hell forever), is of the highest crimes against Almighty God! An interesting fact as follows.

The P.C.A., Presbyterian Church U.S.A. in its "The Book of Confessions" openly states that non-elect infants cannot be saved on page 135, 6.066&6.067 (Westminster Confession of Faith now quoting), ... "Elect infants dying in infancy, are regenerated and saved by Christ…Others, not elected, although they may be called by the ministry of the Word….never come to Christ….and therefore *CANNOT BE SAVED*." Interesting is that while their "Westminster Guardian Angel" makes such edict, the UPCUSA is quick to "interpret" this chapter 10 as follows with a "declarative statement"(which plainly contradicts their sacred Westminster Confession) as follows: page 164, "…..that (statement on pg. 135) is not to be regarded as teaching that any (non elect) who die in infancy are lost. We believe that all dying in infancy are included in the election of grace, and are regenerated and saved by Christ through the Spirit, who works when and where and how he pleases." To say these two statements are not contradictory is plainly dishonest.

Of particular note, is that since Calvinistic doctrine perverts the scripture, "Salvation is of the Lord….." to mean that one cannot "do" anything in regards to their own salvation, then its a wonder any true Calvinist could be saved! Rather than for the unsaved Calvinist take the initiative to humble himself, and repent seeking the Lord for pardon (as the Publican did in Lk. 18:10), he "waits" (so here one can be a Calvinist without being a Christian!?) to see if he is one of the elect for God to make him repent, believe to be saved! How many Calvinists have been lost on this false premise only eternity will tell. (To those who think this author is exaggerating this point, notice the footnote below.) The fact that Jesus "tasted" death for EVERY man, Heb.2:9, **leaves no one out**. This plainly contradicts Calvinism's idea that Jesus died only for the elect! J. Vernon McGee was trained as a Presbyterian, left the church and pastored an independent church for over 20 years. He is quoted as saying (on the 'puritanboard..com/forum) the following:

1. He was discussing chapter 2 and the vanity of toil. He started talking about some people out there who are fatalists, who believe everything is predetermined.

Ecclesiastes 2:11--3:1 (MP3) @ 14:50 in the link below he (McGee) says: ... this man adopts a certain philosophy of life. It's known as fatalism. This was common among the Greeks later on. It's been common among pagans. Buddhism is a fatalistic system. Platonism was. And we find that today, there's certain cults, I won't call them by name, but actually it's fatalism. You gather sometimes the impression that they have a glorious faith in God, but it's fatalism actually, and not really faith in God.

It is claimed that McGee was a 4 point Calvinist. That could be true, we are not completely sure, but credit must be given for the following comment on YouTube:

February 06, 2010 — Dr. McGee calls Calvinism's Doctrine of Election a dangerous and frightful view of God. He also said, if he believed in this doctrine, he'd never attempted to preach the word of God and never try to lead anyone to Christ because there'd be no need of it. 1 Timothy 4:1: Now the Spirit speaketh expressly, that in the latter times some shall depart from the faith, giving heed to seducing spirits, and doctrines of devils; 2 Peter 2:1. But there were false prophets also among the people, even as there shall be false teachers among you, who privily shall bring in damnable heresies, even denying the Lord that bought them, and bring upon themselves swift destruction. 2 Corinthians 11:4 For if he that cometh preacheth another Jesus, whom we have not preached, or if ye receive another spirit, which ye have not received, or another gospel, which ye have not accepted, ye might well bear with him. http://www.thruthebible.org/ Thru the Bible Radio Network

"Calvinism" the Trojan Horse

Reader Note: Harold Camping, on Family Radio, answered a caller's request for guidance on how to be saved with a loud "Not a thing!" He explained that since salvation was "of the Lord," ... and that "believing is a work," .... that man could do nothing to obtain salvation. If he was of the elect, then he would be saved, and if he was not of the elect, there was nothing he could do to get saved, so all he could do was to wait and see if he was of the elect! here again we see the evil of Calvinistic Doctrine. I Tim. 2:3-4. tells us "for this is good and acceptable in the sight of God our Savior, who will have **all** men to be saved and come unto the knowledge of the truth." Calvinists reject the plain word of God!

CHAPTER THREE
Identification with Calvinism

This author has no idea why any born-again Christian, who wisely rejects the false heretical doctrine of Calvin's double predestination, would want to be identified as a Calvinist! One reason seems to be that many teachers and pastors hold that "Calvinism" merely indicates basic belief in the "doctrines of grace" (while they reject unconditional election) as opposed to the Armenian position that works are essential to produce/maintain salvation, so calling themselves "moderate Calvinists." While Calvinism teaches unmerited favor" for our salvation, it certainly perverts the doctrine of the grace of God, by twisting that wonderful doctrine into a perverted gospel! The gospel that God sovereignly chose only a small few to be saved with no regards to their freedom of choice, and as well leaving the rest to go to eternal hell (with no choice of their own) is Calvinism in a nutshell. This makes "moderates" guilty by association!

"Pilgrim Publications" by Bob Ross defines fully the Calvinist meaning of "sovereign grace." A true doctrinally sound soul winner, daily carries a great burden for lost souls, as well as a constant pricking of the heart to win the lost. Calvinism strips away these scriptural burdens and thus allows the Christian to push his responsibility to reach the lost over onto "the sovereignty of God". Yes, this author understands the false Calvinist claim that the sovereignty of God gives him a greater responsibility to win the lost, but this is not the practical truth since whether a sinner goes to hell under his perspective depends, not upon the sinner's choice and our winning him, but whether God divinely "forces by sovereign election the sinner to be saved or not"!

May God help Christians flee being labeled as a Calvinist! The so-called moderate Calvinist has "guilt by association" with heresy!

The Rev. Andrew Wommack of Wommack ministries has written a brief article on the "sovereignty" of God, exposing the misuse and misapplication of that word. Whenever one hears a speaker/pastor/teacher especially emphasizing or pontificating the word/words "sovereign or sovereignty of God" he can pretty well be sure the speaker is a Calvinist. We quote parts of Wommacks excellent article here.

TRUTH ABOUT THE "SOVEREIGNTY" OF GOD BY ANDREW WOMACK

"My heart was really stirred this last month. I attended a meeting where an old friend of mine was ministering. He had been through some terrible things that nearly destroyed his faith. He became bitter and angry at God for the things that had happened. When I heard him, he had humbled himself and was again loving the Lord and excited about the future. Praise the Lord! However, in the process, he had come to believe that it was the Lord that caused all his problems. He had resigned himself to the "sovereignty of God."

I believe this is the worst doctrine in the church today. I know that this is a shocking statement and is near blasphemy to some people, but the way sovereignty" is taught today is a real faith killer. The

Identification with Calvinism

belief that God controls everything that happens to us is one of the devil's biggest inroads into our lives. If this belief is true, then our actions are irrelevant, and our efforts are meaningless. What will be will be. If we believe that God wills everything, good or bad, to happen to us, it gives us some temporary relief from confusion and condemnation, but in the long-term, it slanders God, hinders our trust in God, and leads to passiveness.

The word "sovereign" is not used in the King James Version of the Bible. It is used 303 times in the Old Testament of the New International Version, but it is always used in association with the word "LORD" and is the equivalent of the King James Version's "LORD God." Not a single one of those times is the word "sovereign" used in the manner that it has come to be used in religion in our day and time. Religion has resulted in the invention of a new meaning for the word "sovereign," which basically means God controls everything. Nothing can happen but what He wills or allows. However, there is nothing in the actual definition that states that. The dictionary defines "sovereign" as, "1. Paramount; supreme. 2. Having supreme rank or power. 3. Independent: a sovereign state. 4. Excellent." None of these definitions means that God controls everything.

It is assumed that since God is paramount or supreme that nothing can happen without His approval. That is not what the Scriptures teach. In 2 Peter 3:9, Peter said, "The Lord is...not willing that any should perish, but that all should come to repentance." This clearly states that it is not the Lord's will for anyone to perish, but people are perishing. Jesus said, "Enter ye in at the strait gate: for wide is the gate, and broad is the way, that leadeth to destruction, and many there be which go in thereat" (Matt. 7:13). Relatively few people are saved compared to the number that are lost. God's will for people concerning salvation is not being accomplished. This is because the Lord gave us the freedom to choose. He doesn't will anyone into hell. He paid for the sins of the whole world (1 John 2:2; 1 Tim. 4:10), but we must choose to put our faith in Christ and receive His salvation. People are the ones choosing hell by not choosing Jesus as their Savior. It is the free will of man that damns them, not God.

People virtually have to climb over the roadblocks that God puts in their way to continue on their course to hell. The cross of Christ and the drawing power of the Holy Spirit are obstacles that every sinner encounters. No one will ever stand before God and be able to fault Him for withholding the opportunity to be saved. The Lord woos every person to Him, but we have to cooperate. Ultimately, the Lord simply enforces the consequences of people's own choices. God has a perfect plan for every person's life (Jer. 29:11), but He doesn't make us walk that path. We are free moral agents with the ability to choose. He has told us what the right choices are (Deut. 30:19), but He doesn't make those choices for us. God gave us the power to control our destinies.

Typical teaching on the sovereignty of God puts Jesus in the driver's seat with us as passengers. On the surface that looks good. All of us have encountered the disastrous results of doing our own thing. We desire to be led of the Lord, and the teaching that nothing happens but what God wills fits that nicely. However, the Scriptures paint a picture of each of us being behind the wheel of our own lives. We are the one doing the driving. We are supposed to take directions from the Lord, but He doesn't do the driving for us. Man has been given the authority over his own life, but he must have the Lord's direction to succeed. Jeremiah 10:23 says, "O LORD, I know that the way of man is not in himself: it is not in man that walketh to direct his steps." God created us to be dependent upon Him and our independence is at the root of all our problems. As if it wasn't bad enough for man to try to run his affairs independently of God and His standards, it has been made even worse by religion teaching us that all our problems are actually blessings from God. That is a faith killer. It makes people totally passive.

James 4:7 says, "Submit yourselves therefore to God. Resist the devil, and he will flee from you." This verse makes it clear that some things are from God, and some from the devil. We must submit to the things that are of God and resist the things that are from the devil. The word "resist" means, "Actively fight against." Saying "Whatever will be will be" is not actively fighting against the devil. If a person really believed that God is the one who put sickness on them because He is trying to work something for good in their life, then they should not go to the doctor or take any medicine. That would be resisting God's plans. They should let the sickness run its course and thereby get the full benefit of God's correction. Of course, no one advocates that. That is absurd. It is even more absurd to believe that God is the one behind the tragedy. Acts 10:38 says that Jesus healed all those who were oppressed OF THE DEVIL. It was not God who oppressed them with sickness. It was the devil. It's the same today. Sickness is from the devil, not from God. We need to resist sickness and, by faith, submit ourselves to healing, which is from God through the atonement of Christ.

I know someone is thinking, What about the Old Testament instances where God smote people with sickness and plagues? There is a lot I could say about that if I had the space, but a simplified answer to that question is that none of those instances were blessings. They were curses. God did use sickness in the Old Testament as punishment... both forgiveness of sin and healing are a part of the atonement Jesus provided for us. Deuteronomy, chapter 28, should forever settle this question for all who believe the Word of God. The first 14 verses of Deuteronomy 28 list the blessings of God and the last 53 verses list the curses of God. Healing is listed as a blessing (Deut. 28:4). Sickness is listed as a curse (Deut. 28:22, 27-28, 35, 59-61). God called sickness a curse. We should not call it a blessing. Knowing that God is not the author of my problems is one of the most important revelations the Lord has ever given me. If I thought it was God who killed my father when I was twelve, and some of my best friends before I was 20, if it was God who had people kidnap me, slander me, threaten to kill me, and turn loved ones against me, then I would have a hard time trusting God, if He was like that.

On the contrary, it is very comforting to know that God only has good things in store for me. Any problems in my life are from the devil, of my own making, or just the results of life on a fallen planet. My heavenly Father has never done me any harm and never will. I KNOW that. I am not saying that there is nothing to learn from hardships. Most of you reading this article have come to the Lord because of something in your life that overwhelmed you and caused you to turn to the Lord for help. That situation was not from God regardless of the results. It was you turning to the Lord and the faith you placed in Him that turned your life around, not the hardship. If hardships and problems made us better, then everyone who has had problems would be better for them. Those who have the most trouble would be the best. That simply is not so.

Let me illustrate this with a story about my son, Joshua. When he was only a year old, I was loading lumber on a large truck in the heat of a Texas summer. I had Joshua with me, and he was having

Identification with Calvinism

a big time playing in the lumber yard. By mid-afternoon, he was tired and sleepy and started to lie down in the dirt for a nap. I knew his mother wouldn't like that, so I put him in the cab of the truck to lie down and take his nap. He had been wanting to get into that truck all day, and when I put him in there, he revived. I had to roll the windows down because it was hot, and Joshua was leaning out the windows and waving at me in the side view mirrors. I told him to lie down and even gave him a spanking, but he didn't take heed. He leaned out the window too far, fell out of the cab, hit his eye on the running board and landed on his head. I ran up to him, prayed over him, and held him until he quit crying. Then I told him that was why I told him to lie down and go to sleep and not lean out the window. I used that situation which caused him pain, to teach him, but if Joshua would have been like the sovereignty teachers of today, he would have gone out and told all his friends that his father made him fall out of that truck to teach him to obey. That's not so. I did what I could to restrain him. I would be very hurt if that's the way Joshua thought I was.

Likewise, I don't believe it blesses our heavenly Father for us to blame Him for all the problems that come into our lives. Sure, He will comfort us when we turn to Him in the midst of our problems, but He doesn't create the negative circumstances that hurt our lives. God is sovereign in the sense that He is paramount and supreme. There is no one higher in authority or power, but that does not mean He exercises His power by controlling everything in our lives. God has given us the freedom to choose. He has a plan for us. He seeks to reveal that plan to us and urge us in that direction, but we choose. He doesn't make our choices for us. In many instances, it is our wrong choices that bring disaster upon us. In other cases, our problems are nothing but an attack from the devil. In some cases, natural forces of an imperfect world cause us pain....

This is a fundamental doctrine of Christianity that must be understood properly if you want victory in your life. Believing that God controls everything renders a person passive. Why pray and believe for something better? Whatever God wants will come to pass. That simply is not true. The Lord is the answer to all our problems. He is not the problem. If you would like more ministry on this pivotal point, please order my teaching entitled, "The Sovereignty of God." There is much more detail on the teaching than I was able to put into this article. This teaching will change your life. I suggest that after you listen to it that you share it with someone else. I really believe that confusion on this subject is how Satan pushes his will off on most people. This teaching could change someone's life." (End of Womack Quote).

CHARLES STANLEY AND GOD CONTROLLING ALL THINGS

Does God control all things? Charles Stanley seems to think so. This month, (Nov. 2011) on his television ministry he was declaring the sovereignty of God and that in his belief God was in control of all circumstances. He quoted the well known scripture (Romans 8) that "…and we know that all things work together for good for them that love God and are called according to His purpose." He then proceeded to declare that indeed God is in control of all things and then asked his congregation the following questions. "Are you in control of all things in your life? Who here is?" To which of course no hands were raised. Then he asked, "Well if you are not in control of your life is the Devil?" To which again no hands were raised. Then he asked,

Identification with Calvinism

"Now if Satan is not, and you are not, then is not God in control of all things in your life?" Such preaching no doubt brings great comfort to the saints, but at the same time definitely disarms them to face the realities of life as it comes to them. As well it makes them passive to tolerate conditions and things in their lives which should not be acceptable. Then also, they believe that all things that happen to them are from the hand of, and under the supervision of God! Nothing could be further from the truth. No, absolutely not, God is not in control of all things, though of course He could be, and using this passage of scripture to attempt to prove such a point is not only disgraceful, but dishonest. God is not in control of evil, wickedness, pornography, murder, rape, moral corruption etc, etc. Nor is He in control of satanic attacks upon His people. To say He is in control of all things is an insult to God and His holiness and as well makes Him to be the author of sin (as the Calvinists teach)! First, this verse is not speaking to all people or of all circumstances in the world. It is plainly speaking to "…them that love God and are called according to His purpose." It is speaking to the saved, the redeemed who are walking in the light of righteousness and true holiness. Second, the scripture does not say that God brings all circumstances or 'things' into our lives, but rather that what ever circumstances *are* brought into the life of the redeemed whether good or bad, God can work those circumstances into situations which will bring victory to us and glory to God. Thirdly, it does not say that God is in control of everything that happens to us since Satan himself or his followers can bring circumstances into our lives to damage us and our testimony. There is no doubt that God certainly does bring things into our lives, sometimes blessings, trials and maybe chastisement. While whatever things God brings into our lives is designed to help us, then whatever

"Calvinism" the Trojan Horse

things Satan or his followers bring to us certainly may well harm us and our families, but God can take those things and make their outcome work out for His glory! Yes we may well suffer true damage in our lives from the hand of Satan, but God can in the end, bring healing to us, and honor and glory to Himself. That is of course if we qualify as one who "…loves God and are called according to His purpose." Conversely, that also means if we do not qualify as saved and walking in God's will, then our lives could suffer irreparable damage. The scripture teaches in I John that "…there is a sin unto death" for the believer who becomes enmeshed in certain deadly sin. To those who see Satan's design on Job, which was agreed upon but limited by God as a firm doctrine for us, may well be going to far, since we know not that God has agreed the same for us, but of course could. One day God will indeed be totally in control of all things, but in this present age He is not since were He, sin could not exist. Interesting here, that this latter fact voids the idea that II Thess. 2:7 teaches the Holy Spirit is the restrainer of sin! No, He is not the restrainer of sin but rather is clearly identified in the gospel of John 16:8-11 as the One who "…convicts the world of sin, righteousness and judgment." As stated, if He were the restrainer of sin, then He would do a perfect job of restraining sin, and no sin could exist or occur! If the Holy Spirit were sent to 'restrain sin' then He could not do less than a perfect job! God cannot fail at anything He does.

Should not a Christian call himself a "Calvinist" because most Christians hold that salvation is by grace (unmerited favor), and Calvinists claim to preach the "doctrines of grace?" To answer that, we ask the following question. Should this author call himself a "Russellite" because there are a number of doctrines he holds identical to the Watchtower? (i.e. The virgin birth, bodily resurrection of

Christ, new heaven and earth, One God etc?) Absolutely not! The Watchtower denies the Deity of our Savior! Thus why should any Christian call himself a "Calvinist" when Calvin taught "another gospel"? As well, I do not know any born again Christian who denies the Sovereignty of God so there can be no excuse for anyone to be called a "Calvinist". The Satanic ploy to make Calvinism more palatable to unsuspecting Christians is to say that Calvinism is merely the doctrine of the "Sovereign Grace of God" in salvation. Now what Bible believing Christian does not believe that? Calvinism on the other hand perverts that precious truth into the false doctrine of forced salvation and forced damnation, i.e. fatalism!

"Calvinism" the Trojan Horse

"CALVINIST REVIVAL OF DEADNESS EXPLANATION THEREOF FOLLOWING

Preaching Calvinism in any church ushers in a spirit of deadness, and a true lack of con-cern for the lost, stripping away any sense of urgency to win the unsaved. Calvinism clearly implies that absolutely no one is in danger of going to hell. The clear implication is that the elect being elected from before the foundation of the world (even if they are at present lost and not saved yet), eventually will undoubtedly be saved, and thus never are in any danger, while the non-elect must go to hell without ever any hope. If never any hope then, they could never be said to ever be in any "danger" of going to hell since they cannot go anywhere else. For someone to be "in danger of going to hell" clearly implies that there is a possibility of not having to go there, which certainly according to Calvinism could not apply to the non-elect. Worse yet if Calvin's brand of election is true are we to believe Jesus lied by warning all unsaved to avoid going to hell at all costs in order to precipitate salvation for the elect?! Who are we to believe, Jesus or Calvin?

PRESBYTERIANISM BAPTISM AND INFANT REGENERATION

Presbyterian theologian G.I. Williamson in his "The Westminster Confession of Faith for Study Classes" page 207, ch.20 reveals that Presbyterians do indeed see baptism as a sacrament denoting regeneration and union to Christ. He says.... "Baptism signifies,

1. Admission into the visible Church,
2. The grace of the covenant,
3. Regeneration,
4. The remission of sins, and
5. The duty of new obedience.

It is a sign and seal, not of this or that part of a certain great work of divine grace, but of the whole complex wonder of it. Baptism is, as it were a great "motion picture," which shows forth that great work of God whereby dead sinners are brought into living union with Christ, and with God. And the central concept expressed by baptism is this union itself. The baptismal formula recorded in Matt.28:19 shows this quite clearly. Believers and their children *(identified also as infants bottom page 209)* are to be baptized into the name of the Father and of the Son and of the Holy Ghost… **And so it is with those who are baptized into relationship with the triune God.**" (End of Williamson quote.) Certainly it is clear reading chapter 26 that Presbyterians hold to "elect infant regeneration" at or some time before the time of baptism. Interesting to note with this that he is quick to say on page 215 (somewhat contradictory to say the least) that…….. "Baptism never causes union with Christ. It never has is not to effect union with Christ but rather to confirm and testify such." Naturally here enters the doctrine of election….i.e. some babies are elect, and some are not….thus the elect babies become regenerated at or sometime before the time of baptism.

Presbyterians see regeneration not as conversion and salvation/new birth as we Baptist do, but rather the implanting of the seeds of repentance and faith which will (they say) eventually years later germinate into conversion and the new birth. (G.I. Williamson confirms this in his W.M.C.of Faith for study classes.)

Calvinism certainly is a serious blight on Biblical Christianity. Usually it is the pastor or seminary student which Satan targets to become ensnared in the meshes of this deadly heresy that their soul winning zeal will erode away. Parishioners usually are completely oblivious to the basic doctrinal stand of their individual local churches, a sad fact indeed.

Identification with Calvinism

Following are reasons why "Calvinists-Reformed" pastors and or college/seminary professors are NOT qualified to minister the Word of God and should be made to resign from evangelical institutions. (Calvinism is not tolerated at Midwestern Baptist College, Pontiac, Mich. Any Calvinists which surface there are plainly told to "leave now.")

1. Calvinism in reality represents God as being the author and originator of sin, though naturally many Calvinists deny this. BUT...their "Westminster Confession...." Page125 says...."God from all eternity...ordains whatsoever comes to pass...etc." If "whatsoever" means what it should mean...then that includes all sinful actions and acts of rebellion!

2. Calvinists claim that God ordained all thoughts, actions and deeds which must necessarily therefore come to pass including the choice to accept or reject salvation.

3. Calvinists usually are not strong personal soul winners, so they are therefore poor examples to the flock for leadership in doing the same.

4. Calvinists look upon the lost/unchurched as being permanently locked in as either elect, or non-elect. i.e. All predestined for hell or heaven no matter what or how he preaches or teaches. Thus their incentive to "rescue the perishing" is seriously eroded away.

5. Calvinists are many times "closet Calvinists." The basic idea that "God would create conscious living souls who have no choice of their own, no free will of their own, to choose their destiny either in heaven or hell,

and then he (God) would choose only a small minority to escape the fires of hell, while forcing the remaining majority to be tormented in a burning hell for all of eternity creates a monstrous God totally foreign to the Word of God. Now how many Presbyterian/Baptist/reformed (etc) Pastors would come forward to their congregations to admit to embracing that theology?

6. Calvinist Pastors enjoy having people look up to and revere them as "men of the cloth" and are NOT so burdened with the responsibility of "rescuing the perishing" as are their fellow non-Calvinist pastor friends. I can hear the cry.... "But they are good men, and though not perfect they love their congregations". To this needs only be the scriptural reply...Galatians 1:8...."If any man preach any other gospel than that ye have received let him be ACCURSED!" (I suppose it is true that a pastor who "believes the doctrines of Calvin" but does not teach it, has far less guilt here). The simple fact is that if the Calvinists are correct in their theology, then those of us who believe that anyone can be saved, and for that reason all need to be preached to, are the ones preaching "another gospel". Sorry it cannot be both ways.

7. Calvinism is plainly "another gospel," certainly not the wonderful gospel of the Bible where Jesus came to offer free salvation to ALL men, women, boys, and girls. To represent Calvinism is not to represent the Word of Almighty God!

Identification with Calvinism

This author was going to write a rather extensive booklet further exposing Calvinism, but the Lord has seen fit to relegate that task to "Dave Hunt"… who has written a thoroughly devastating expose on Calvinism named, "What Love Is This" published by, "Loyal Publishing Inc., P.O. Box 1892, Sisters OR. 97759. This book almost 500 pages, is absolutely irrefutable, and shows also the hideous other side of John Calvin as he ruled Geneva, with the hand of a Protestant Pope. Torturing, putting people to death/ and banishing those who dare to teach/preach/or believe anything else than his false system of theology. This book is a must! That the hands of Calvinists drip guilty with the blood of lost souls is evident from their theology. Ezekiel warns that if the righteous fail to warn/win the wicked (the non-elected yet) of their lost sinful condition then they (the righteous) will be accomplices in guilt against the gospel by the wicked unsaved! An interesting note is that these several chapters in Ezekiel Ch.18&33, when read carefully totally contradicts the basic doctrines of Calvin. Note also that God holds the "**wicked**" responsible for their damnation and not His sovereign election!

My prayer is that evangelical churches will find out if their pastor is a Calvinist, particularly if he believes in "Unconditional Election" (forced salvation and forced damnation) and if so force his resignation. God help our churches to be free from this blasphemous deadening influence! (An interesting note here is when John Calvin ruled Geneva attempting to force by law all of his subjects to bow to his theology, then if people are "elected according to his definition" the question naturally arises why should anyone be forced to become a Calvinist without knowing if he or she is elect or not! He attempted and forced by law, persecution, threat of exile and possible death to citizens of Geneva to bow to his theological position. The question

"Calvinism" the Trojan Horse

therefore arises… is that the means Jesus used to win men to himself? Jesus said "Whosoever will let Him come and drink of the water of life freely".

Jesus never persecuted anyone or attempted to force anyone to come to himself. Dave Hunt's book "What Love Is This" is a must to read, validating Calvin's Protestant Popery.

Only three options? So say the Calvinists. The idea is if you are not a Calvinist you must be an Armenian or a Universalist. This author thanks the Lord that there is an alternative….simply being a Bible believing Christian who believes Jesus died for all men and offers to all men free permanent salvation upon their repentance and faith in Christ. Many men have been turned away from Christ by the "Calvinistic hell fire/brimstone" type theology which says that God has already determined who will be saved and who will be lost, and those not sovereignly elected (forced to be saved) will be tormented in hell for eternity. What a monstrous God that is! Certainly that is the God of "Reformed Calvinistic" theology and as defined in the "Westminster Confession of (*Heresy –ed.*) Faith.

The scriptures are plain to teach that God is not willing that any should perish, but that all should come to repentance and acknowledgement of the truth! 2Pet.3:9. Yes certainly there is a real hell, but only those who refuse God's free offer of salvation will be there forever! The Calvinist is quick to piously proclaim that "God is in control of all things." Parishioners sit ignorantly (and sleepily) nodding in agreement saying "amen". Sorry…..that doctrine is false.

This Calvinist doctrine of fatalistic theology has seeped into most theological circles, and surprisingly enough through devotional literature. The false idea that "God is in control of all things" is a major offshoot from the idea that God is responsible for double predestination in the salvation or damnation of all. No! God is NOT in control of all things! Of course God could be 100% in control of all things, of course one day He will be, of course there are certain things that God is in control of, and of course His power is not limited to be in control of all things! Now however, during man's probationary existence in this life God has not been in control of sin, of the mafia, of rape, murder, Hitler's carnage, depravity and wicked acts of men and nations!

The Calvinists seem to think so, i.e. that "God has ordained all things that come to pass." That God "permits" sin, akin to "giving or issuing a permit" for man to sin! That God is "in control of all things." No! God does not, nor ever has given His nod of approval for man to sin, or nod for permission for man to sin! That is on Satan who is the "god of this world!" God is not the "God of this world and in control of this world," Satan is the "god of this world, and is temporarily in control of this world!" IICor.4:3-4.

Reading Oswald Chambers daily devotional material for June 13, in "My Utmost for His Highest." Under the title, "Getting There," he states as follows; "…a saint realizes that it is God who engineers his circumstances." Sorry…that is not true. Yes God does indeed engineer many circumstances in our lives, but Satan indeed does attack and engineer many problems in the Christian's walk through this life of trial and adversity. The Calvinist type theology endeavors to lull the Christian into a false sense of security, and accept everything that comes into his life as being "God's will." Certainly this author knows that God can take any circumstances we are in and turn them around for good in the end, as Romans 8:28 clearly teaches. "But"…the saint needs to be wary….to be vigilant…..for Satan, "walks to and fro in the earth seeking whom he may devour."

How many Christians living under this false sense of security eventually become disheartened and discouraged when living with this false conception. They slip back into waywardness and disbelief when their life comes crashing down around them! Many have become disillusioned and disappointed that damage has come to them or their families when they were "trusting the Lord" that "all circumstances that befell them were under control of God!" Christians must therefore be ready to "resist the Devil", "to arm themselves," to "do battle with the forces of evil" to watch and pray lest they "be brought into a place of temptation!" Thus a far cry from the passive, inactive response of the Calvinist theology which can lead Christians to defeat and ruin!

THE HIDEOUSLY CRUEL GOD OF CALVINISM

For Almighty God to be portrayed as a God who totally sovereignly "elects" (thus forces) only a "few" precious souls to be saved and enter the portals of heaven for eternity, and thus "non-elects" (forces) the majority of humanity to go to and painfully suffer in an eternal burning hell for ever and ever is to portray a God that is a sadistic, cruel, vicious God! Isn't it strange that such a God could have decided to "elect" all mankind, and thus force all mankind to bend their knee and glorify himself in delivering all of them from that burning hell?

The unwitting inference of Calvinism is just that....that God could have "forced" all to be saved and have 100% glory by causing all to be saved, rather than have say only 20-30% to be saved giving Him only partial glory. For anyone to defend that kind of theological view of God/Christ, or defend pastors who hold such Calvinist positions, are certainly apostate in their doctrine. For any professing Christian to say it doesn't matter if the plan of salvation is changed from "whosoever will" as the Bible teaches, to "whosoever is forced to be saved" as Calvinism teaches will one day stand before God and give account for endorsing apostasy.

SATAN AND GOD THE SAME?

Calvinism unwittingly makes mockery of the need for forgiveness, the incarnation and the reason there of! Scripture is plain, that the Word of God was made flesh (Jn.1:14) to offer sinful man reconciliation and forgiveness through the shed blood of Christ. How is one to believe that "man" needs to be "forgiven" when Calvinism teaches that God planned, ordained, and caused man to enter temptation, or yea that God ordained that man should fall! Calvin taught that God deemed it meet that man should fall (i.e. should commit sin worthy of eternal damnation!). Thus… Almighty God is being charged by Calvinism with being the author and originator of sin. Calvinism thus infers that "God" would be the guilty one, guilty of intending/ causing/ planning for innocent man to sin! (Would this not make God and Satan equals in their design for man to sin and fail, and how could man need forgiveness for what "God" [and Satan??] caused/ planned for him to do?) This false charge is the same as for someone to deliberately stumble a weak invalid person causing them to break a leg, and then offer them medical help if they show sorrow for stumbling and falling down! Notice as follows Calvin's convoluted reasoning:

Calvin and God Intending for Man to Sin
Book 3:8 chapter 23: (Institutes): "…Predestination is…a secret indeed, but unblameable, because it is certain that the destruction consequent upon predestination is also most just. Moreover, though

their (man's, ed.) perdition depends on the predestination of God, the cause and matter of it is in themselves. The first man fell because the Lord deemed it meet that he should: why He deemed it meet we know not. It is certain, however that it was just (i.e. "justified" ed.) because He saw that His own glory would thereby be displayed." (And further, book 3:7). "Nor ought it to seem absurd when I say, that God not only foresaw the fall of the first man, and in him the ruin of his posterity; but also at his own pleasure arranged it."

Now the above quotations from Calvin's institutes plainly show the foolish and unreasonable conclusions Calvin promotes. Not only that but these conclusions are not supported by one shred of scripture from Gen.1:1 to Rev. 22:21! Notice as follows the false doctrines manufactured by the unscriptural reasoning of Augustinian/Calvinism.

1. The reason people are predestined to different fates, some to heaven and some to hell is unknown and thus a secret known only to God. Interesting here that what Calvin claims to be known only to God is revealed to HIMSELF! "...that His own glory would be displayed." Here Calvin claims an extra Biblical insight thus adding to the Word of God! How, in the name of God Almighty, does God get glory, planning and intending for innocent man to fail and sin, and then only "predestinating a few to escape to heaven for eternity while damning the rest/majority to burn in eternal hell?! That glorifies God??

2. Predestination of the non-elect to eternal hell fire, according to Calvin here, is "just" or "deserved" by the reprobated because the "cause of it" is "in them."

What is that "cause" in them? Plainly he says that the cause in them is "…that His glory would thereby be displayed." i.e. Innocent man becomes guilty of committing sin worthy of burning in hell for eternity because God secretly wanted to display His glory and thereby caused, planned and arranged for man to sin (his words)! So here we have Calvin's God a. Wanting to be glorified by His creation. b. Causing an innocent man to sin and bring his posterity to ruin. c. Selecting/electing and causing only a small few to be eventually saved. d. Causing the rest of humanity to burn and suffer in eternal hell fire because He for His own reasons not known to us (except of course to Calvin, "that God be glorified"), passed them by and did not elect them causing them to become the non-elect and reprobated to hell. This false charge naturally makes God the author and originator of all of mankind's sins, and therefore the death of Jesus on the cross for our sins was because God wanted Him to suffer and die for our sins. Sins which He planned and arranged for man to commit!

Certainly, no student of the Word of God can endorse the above as Biblical Christianity! One needs only to read the first several chapters of Genesis, and the fall of man to see how plainly this contradicts the Word of God. Calvinism must be rejected. Hmmm, this author wonders now if Calvinism is really trying to teach that the serpent tempting Eve was God in disguise intending and arranging for man to sin and fall in the Garden of Eden? One in the same??? Did not

"Calvinism" the Trojan Horse

God clearly reveal His will/command by spoken word when He said "Thou shalt not eat of it (the tree of knowledge of good and evil) for in the day thou eatest thereof thou shalt surely die." Gen. 2:16-17. For God to "plan and arrange for man to sin" and then command him not to is to accuse God of wickedness, and of violation of His desire for man's innocence in wanting man to sin that He be glorified !!!.

Think also, if God did plan and arrange for man to sin, then that would be the same as for a godly Christian father to plan and arrange for his innocent pure son to have sex with a prostitute to bring ruin, shame, disease upon him and his posterity. As well he does this to receive honor, gratitude and thanks, when later he causes his son to beg his forgiveness for his failure! An insane accusation!

Footnote: While D.J. Kennedy may well be credited with his "Evangelism Explosion" book (a manual for Presbyterian techniques in winning men to Christ), it is interesting to note in the book that he teaches NOT to ask a person if he is saved.(page 57 pgh.3. He states "… are you saved is repugnant" and couples that with accosting someone grabbing the unsaved by the lapels at the same time! This attitude is certainly repugnant to the Bible where Paul plainly rejoices that… "The preaching of the cross is to them that perish foolishness, but unto us which are SAVED is the power of God!" I Cor. 1:18) It is this authors opinion that his Calvinism forbids this approach since according to Calvinism it is not up to us whether or not we are saved, but rather up to God and his election of "some to salvation" and therefore "some to damnation". Not only that but this author finds it offensive that a Calvinist such as he should seem to place a claim of promoting evangelism for all men, when Calvin and his doctrines plainly contradict that idea by their doctrines of the infamous heretical "TULIP"! I think it interesting that no Calvinist would dare stand in the pulpit (or in his supposed witnessing) and tell his listeners…. "Some of you are elected to be saved and some of you are therefore forced to go to hell by not being elected since it is not up to you if you are saved or not!" This author has been soul winning for over 40 years, door to door, on streets, and in every possible situation and have asked countless people…. "Are you saved?" with wonderful results…results of winning men to Christ, and yes seeing many refuse to come to salvation but not because I asked them if they were saved or not! Interesting that Kennedy while being a Calvinist holds man to be 100% responsible for his lost condition. Page 123 in "Evangelism Explosion".... "The Bible says that man broke this relationship-that he and God were one together, but that they were separated from each other. They were separated because man got out of tune with God, He rebelled against God's perfect will and direction for his life." Now this plainly contradicts the W.M.C. of Faith in which it says as already stated earlier in this paper, that "God....ordained all things which come to pass." Pages 127, 125, 133, and 87 show he does indeed use "danger of going to hell' in his witnessing in total contradiction to fatalistic Calvinism as discussed also earlier. Sorry... Calvinist cannot have it both ways, but they do try to in order to appear "mainstream fundamental to the Word of God"!

"Calvinism" the Trojan Horse

"THE NON ELECT AT WORK" EXPLANATION THEREOF FOLLOWING

Calvin's false idea that God has reprobated most of humanity to be lost and go to hell, yea and intended for them to sin and be forever lost is shown here. If the unsaved after attending church discover they are "non-elect" then what else should they do? Should they live a clean moral straight life hoping for a "lighter punishment" in hell forever, or go out filling every desire of the sinful flesh since they were "passed over" by God and therefore forced to be totally depraved and reprobated to be lost as Calvin taught? If Calvinism were true, then no wonder if the "non-elect" are angry at God for refusing to give them a chance to be saved! The question naturally comes to mind, "How many poor souls have there been in past cen-turies, who have lived and died believing Calvinism, but have regarded themselves as "non-elect" due to their hopeless enslavement or love for sin?" No doubt that false doctrine has bred in them the absolutely worst attitudes (and sins) against God and the church. Certainly here, only the non Calvinist can offer that suffering lost soul unconditional love, sure salvation and liberation from their life of sin where Calvinism clearly falls short! Shockingly, Calvinism teaches the following:

CALVINS INSTITUTES, BOOK 3, 23:12 QUOTING JOHN CALVIN:

"Another argument which they (unbelievers in Calvin's type election. ed.) employ to overthrow predestination is, that if it stand, all care and study of well doing must cease. For what man can hear (say they) that life and death are fixed by an eternal and immutable decree of God, without immediately concluding that it is of no consequence how he acts, since no work of his can either hinder or further the predestination of God? **Thus all will rush on and like desperate men plunge headlong wherever lust inclines.** *And it is true* **that this is not altogether a fiction; for there are multitudes of a swinish nature who define their doctrine of predestination** *("their doctrine" being "their doctrine of being predestinated to be lost/damned with no hope" ed.)* By their profane blasphemies, and employ them as a cloak to evade all admonition and censure. "God knows what he has determined to do with regard to us; if he has decreed our salvation, he will bring us to it in his own time; if he has doomed us to death (hell. Ed.) It is vain for us to fight against it." Author: John Calvin.

CHAPTER FOUR
Proposed Litmus Test

Following is a proposed Litmus test for all pastors and Christian workers applying for positions in our evangelical churches. To place a Calvinist in a place of leadership/teaching/preaching in our churches is to desecrate that holy office and calling, and, as well, bring possible stagnation and ruin to the church. Five simple questions, the pulpit committee could easily ask a candidate would prevent such occurrence. It is this authors firm conviction that "Calvinist pastoral candidates" will likely do everything possible to hide their true beliefs hedging questions from a pulpit committee and the church, if the church is not a "reformed/Calvinistic type church, very deceitful indeed.

Proposed Litmus Test for All Pastors and Christian Workers

1. Do you believe a predetermined number of people were selected (elected) by God from before the foundation of the world to be saved and that the reason for their election was not their forseen repentance and conversion, but rather that "God according to his sovereign pleasure elected those whom he so chose? Yes or No?

2. If yes to the preceeding question then you accept the doctrine of John Calvin of Unconditional election, is that correct? Yes or No?

3. Do you also accept the other points of Calvin namely the "TULIP"? Yes or No?

4. Do you believe that the souls which do go to hell, could never have been saved since God did not sovereignly elect them? Yes or No?

5. If Jesus came to seek and to save the "lost" then that makes the lost the elect. so then, that must make the "non-elect" not lost since the spiritual condition of the "non-elect is opposite that of the "elect"! so....... if the non-elect are lost then Jesus must seek them as well, and if not lost then universal salvation would be true thus contradicting calvinism either way! Yes or No?

Now a true Calvinist will answer questions 1-4 in the affirmative, and the last question should show him the absurdity of his position.

Statement: God intended for man to sin? Now if this is not a plain satanic assault upon the integrity of the Lord, then I do not know what it is! God cannot be charged with sin, nor can He be charged with "causing man to sin". "Intending" or "Causing" man to sin is one in the same. Calvinists have gone to far here in their offence of Almighty God. Should this author, lock a young man in a room with a prostitute, give a bottle of alcoholic beverage to a group of underage teens, give a loaded gun to a convicted felon with a map of the local bank, etc., I am sure that any sane person would say I was setting up those mentioned for a fall into sin, and thus make myself responsible for stumbling someone into sin. Now should God be charged with doing the same? "Intending for man to sin?"

Certainly the Calvinists pervert the doctrine of the sovereignty of God into that which is perversely against the Bible the Word of God! This author has no sympathy for those bleeding heart parishioners/pastors etc, which say that "We all have our own views on theology and we are all trying to get to the same place. Certainly the scriptures are plain to teach (contrary to Calvinism) that all men are candidates for salvation and eternal life in Christ, and it is our commission as Christians to "Win the Lost At Any Cost." Romans 10:13, "For whosoever shall call upon the name of the Lord shall be saved."

The Calvinist needs to be asked.... "Saved from what?" Romans 10:13 has absolutely no meaning if Calvinism is true! If someone is lost and one of the elect, then that one need not worry about being saved since he is in no danger of ever going to hell. The "non elect" need not be warned since according to Calvinism they are reprobated to hell and have no hope of salvation anyway.

Therefore the simple truth in a nutshell is that "no one" needs to worry in the least about going to hell. The unsaved have no idea if they are "elect" or not, since according to Calvin it is not up to them if they are finally saved or not, so all they need to do is live their lives daily and wait to see if the salvation of God "comes to them". Of course if the Church is supposed to preach that Jesus Christ came to save some, i.e. the elect, then the lost sinner is really in no danger of going to hell if he is one of the elect. The reprobated to hell need not be warned since they cannot possibly be saved anyway.

Thus, Calvinism makes all the warnings of the Bible about the terrors of hell and the lake of fire nothing more than LIES since no one is really in danger of going there, and again the reprobated to hell have to go there anyway so they need not be warned to repent! When Calvinists teach that we are to warn all men of hell since we do not know who are elect or not, in reality says that we are to preach a "false threat" or a "lie" in order to make the unsaved repent and be saved. I am sure that God would never approve of preaching a lie to excite men to be saved.

To offer salvation to all people, supposedly knowing that only a small elect group are to be saved, is the same as a Captain of a rescue ship offering just a "few" life boats to a sinking ship of people who are mostly invalid and paraplegics, while others on the ship have been enabled by the Captain to be strong and able to get into the life boats, and do so leaving the weak and infirmed behind! Now would not the world be outraged at the Captain for not using his full capabilities to rescue all of the rest of the weak and infirmed? Would the Captain have pleasure that he rescued the strong and enabled persons, while "sovereignly deciding" to leave the weak and infirmed to perish at sea? (Calvinists teach that God chooses certain souls to be saved solely on the basis of Divine pleasure and sovereignty. See #18 following under "Pernicious Theology")

If "Divine pleasure was the basis of election to salvation then God would be obligated to elect and save **all** that His pleasure not be violated by willingly leaving many weak and infirmed to perish when he could have caused them to be saved also! So has not God the ability to "enable, and strengthen" **all** men so that all have the power to come to Christ and be saved? Certainly he does and can (of course Calvinists teach God enables, strengthens and draws only select few to be saved), but that does not mean all men will choose to be saved. Many refuse from different excuses.

God is not willing that any should perish but that all men should come to repentance.

II Pet.3:9 To say the Holy Spirit only enables a small few to be

Proposed Litmus Test

saved, leaving the majority of the world to perish in their sin and go to burn in torments in a fiery hell for eternity, is to unwittingly endorse gross discrimination against the weak and helpless! (Remember Calvinists say that God must enable the sinner in every way to come be saved, and they are totally helpless to seek God/Christ in any way on their own).

Thankfully however, any unsaved person, can pick up the Bible, read it, and follow God's command to repent and believe on Jesus Christ by faith and be saved! (Sad Calvinism does not teach this). Certainly any "god" that is considered loving and kind, no matter what religion, would take great pleasure in helping the disabled, weak, infirmed, and the blind have access to a door leading them out of their misery. Are not all lost sinners disabled, weak, infirmed and blind according to God's word? Certainly, and the difference between Calvinism and the Bible is that, according to Calvinism, God chooses only to help a small few "elect" out of their miseries, while shutting that same avenue of exit to all the rest of humanity.

The Bible on the other hand teaches that God provides enlightenment to All men, and enables All to be saved if they so choose. John tells us that "Jesus Christ is the light that lightest every man that cometh into the world" Jn.1:9. Then 1 Tim.4:10 "...Jesus Christ is the Savior of all men especially of those that believe."

Take another simple example. A fireman at the scene of a fire at an orphanage full of invalid weak helpless children has the full capacity and strength to save all the children from perishing in the fire. He however, according to his pleasure, and sovereignty, decides to save only 35% of the children knowing that the 35% will give him great glory for their salvation from the fire, and give him praise and adulation forever. So... he does just that leaving the other 65% to

"Calvinism" the Trojan Horse

be lost and painfully perish in the fire. According to Calvinism since "God ordained all things that come to pass" so that would make the fireman the one who planned for, and intended for the fire to start!!

Thus a perfect parallel with Calvinism. That fireman would certainly go to court for dereliction of duty, and probably would be convicted of voluntary homicide in not rescuing all from perishing when he could have saved them all. Now what sane person in the world would give him praise and adulation for saving the 35% while leaving the others to perish? But this is the God of Calvinism! (Upon relating this "fireman" parallel with a Calvinist acquaintance of mine, the Calvinist said, "Well I am not that kind of Calvinist!" but in reality ALL Calvinists are "that kind of Calvinists". Any one who calls himself a Calvinist believes in "Unconditional Election" AND THUS IS INDEED that kind of Calvinist. They simply do not understand the true implication of their leaders [John Calvin's] apostate doctrines!). The God of the Bible, on the other hand gives all a way of escape, and offers salvation to all people, and all can be saved if they repent of their sins and trust Jesus. To say as Calvin says that election was strictly according to the "good pleasure and sovereignty of God" is to impugn, malign, and desecrate the character of God and as well bring the death of Jesus Christ and His shed blood into disrepute. Yes there certainly is an eternal hell, and those who reject Jesus Christ will certainly go there if they do not trust Him and be saved.

The simple fact is, Calvinism is "another Gospel" certainly not the Gospel of Christ and must be exposed as such. It would only be fair to say that the "gospel" John Knox (as well as Calvin) wanted to spread in his native land (to supplant Roman Catholicism), was the "gospel" of the sovereignty of God in electing whomsoever He would according to His "good pleasure" as opposed to the "gospel of free salvation *offered to all men thereby giving all men the possibility of being saved.* (The difference of course in this case was that the Roman Catholic Church was offering their slant on salvation to all men i.e. "salvation thru the Church of Rome by good works")..

KNOX AND CALVIN

This author finds it interesting, that a double standard seems to exist between leadership qualifications today and the qualifications of their founders. Suppose if a pastor were to stand before a pulpit committee today and say the following: *"I am candidating for position as pastor of this church but must admit the following. I find nothing in me but vantiy and corruption. I am negligent in being quiet, when in trouble I am impatient tending to desperation. Pride and ambition covetousness and malice constantly trouble me on the other, so that the flesh almost suppresses the work of the Spirit."* Now, knowing the Word of God in Galatians 5 which says, "Now the fruit of the Spirit is love, joy, peace, longsuffering, gentleness, goodness, faith, meekness, temperance against such there is no law, but the works of the flesh are manifest which are, adultery, uncleanness, fornication, lasciviousness, idolatry witchcraft, hatred variance, emulations, wrath, stife, seditions, heresies, envyings, murders, drunkeness, revellings". I would like to know what church would accept such afore admission of depravity in a pastoral candidate as an acceptable leader? Since the scripture plainly says there that those with such fleshly traits are not going to inherit the kingdom of God (vs.22), then how pray tell, could a pastoral candidate with such raging traits be accepted?

Can it be believed here that John Knox (Calvinist and a founder of the Presbyterian Church) while fellowshipping with a Jesuit admitted such internal depravity to the same?

Quoting Mark Bubeck in "The Adversary"... "John Knox the great Scottish reformer, was one of God's noblest servants and one of the most deeply spiritual men the world has ever known. In the year he died, John Knox wrote these words to his 'Answer to a letter of James Lurie, a Scottish Jesuit.' He wrote,

> Now after many battles, I find nothing in me but vantiy and corruption. For in quietness I am negligent, in trouble impatient, tending to desperation;....pride and ambition assault me on the one part, covetousness and malice trouble me on the other; briefly, Oh Lord, the affections of the flesh do almost suppress the operation of Thy Spirit.... In none of the aforesaid I do delight; but I am troubled, and that sore against the desire of my inward man which sobs for my corruption, and would repose in thy mercy alone..." (The Adversary by Mark Bubeck. Page 33).

It would be wise to take notice, as some have not, that the Jesuits were/are strong followers of the Pope! Imagine, confessing such internal depravity (a church standard for Calvinist leaders today?) to a Roman Catholic Priest who is totally dedicated to the Pope and his heresies! What is/was a Jesuit? Notice as follows:

-SOCIETY OF JESUS-

From Wikipedia, the free encyclopedia
   (Redirected from Jesuit)
   Jump to: navigation, search

Seal of the Society of Jesus. The "IHS" trigram comprises the first three Greek letters of "ΙΗΣΟΥΣ" (Jesus), later interpreted as "Iesus Hominum Salvator", *Jesus, Saviour of Mankind*, "Iesum Habemus Socium", *We have Jesus as Companion* or as "Iesu Humilis Societas", *Humble Society of Jesus*

The Society of Jesus (Latin: Societas Iesu, S.J. and S.I. or SJ, SI) is a Catholic religious order of clerks regular whose members are called Jesuits, Soldiers of Christ, and Foot soldiers of the Pope, because the founder, Saint Ignatius of Loyola, was a knight before becoming a priest.

Jesuits are the largest male religious order in the Catholic Church, with 18,815 members — 13,305 priests, 2,295 scholastic students, 1,758 brothers and 827 novices — as of January 2008,

This group bound themselves by a vow of poverty and chastity, to "enter upon hospital and missionary work in Jerusalem, or to go without questioning wherever the pope might direct". (For the "Blood Oath" of the Jesuits see "satanismexposed.org" very shocking indeed. The Jesuits were also to be spies, traitors, betrayers and persecuters even unto death of any opposers of the Pope! Ed.).

In 1540 Ignatius Loyola, a Spanish Priest founded the army/order of the Jesuits. The "**secret**" oath of the Jesuits to serve the Pope according to his pleasure, along with Loyola's vitriolic hatred of the doctrines of Grace, inevitably would lead to the Jesuit mission to effect a "counter-reformation" by declaring war on the true Christian faith. This mission is reflected in this excerpt of the Jesuit oath:

> "I furthermore promise and declare that I will, when opportunity present, make and wage relentless war, secretly or openly, against all heretics, Protestants and Liberals, as I am directed to do, to extirpate and exterminate them from the face of the whole earth; and that I will spare neither

age, sex or condition; and that I will hang, waste, boil, flay, strangle and bury alive these infamous heretics, rip up the stomachs and wombs of their women and crush their infants' heads against the walls, in order to annihilate forever their execrable race. That when the same cannot be done openly, I will secretly use the poisoned cup, the strangulating cord, the steel of the poniard or the leaden bullet, regardless of the honor, rank, dignity, or authority of the person or persons, whatever may be their condition in life, either public or private, as I at any time may be directed so to do by any agent of the Pope or Superior of the Brotherhood of the Holy Faith, of the Society of Jesus".(Quotation from http://www.swrb.com/Puritan/calvinism.htm)

Certainly Knox had a tremendous impact in the Protestant Reformation. Knox accused the Catholic clergy of Scotland of being "gluttons, wantons and licentious revelers, but who yet regularly and meekly partook of the sacrament. Unfortunately, Knox traveled to Geneva three times to study under Calvin who had a high regard for the young Scotsman. Amazing it is that Bubeck also proclaims that Knox was "…..one of the most deeply spiritual men the world has ever known." (!?).

Thus when the Calvinist talks of Knox preaching the gospel, that gospel is the one of Calvin or Unconditional Election, or of forced salvation or forced damnation, certainly not the gospel of the Bible where salvation is offered to all as in John 3:16. Certainly this gospel is slowly being replaced by Calvin and his followers!"

ROMAN CATHOLIC CREDIBILITY?

This author finds it amazing that Roman Catholicism has gained such credibility in supposedly Bible believing Christian circles and by ministers such as Dr. Jack Van Impe, since the Council of Trent decrees in the 1500's proclaimed and still does that there is no salvation outside of the Roman Catholic Church, and all who die outside the Church of Rome are eternally damned to burn in hell! Certainly the doctrine of denominational salvation lies here. Also as well, this year, this author has heard the Rev. Billy Graham bring praise in passing in a sermon to Mother Teresa and as well to Augustine! Having already commented on Augustine, it is well to remember that while Mother Teresa did many good works, she was a Roman Catholic Nun in full and good standing in an apostate church. It doesn't matter? Please notice as follows:

Notable quotes from "Mother" Teresa (12/4/89 Time , pp. 11 & 13):(a) "The dying, the crippled, the mentally ill , the unwanted, the unloved—they are Jesus in disguise . ... [through the] poor people I have an opportunity to be 24 hours a day with Jesus." [On another occasion, she again demonstrated her pantheistic religious philosophy: "Every AIDS victim is Jesus in a pitiful disguise; Jesus is in everyone ... [AIDS sufferers are] children of God [who] have been created for greater things" (1/13/86 Time).](b) "You must make them feel loved and wanted. They are Jesus for me."(c) "I love all religions. ... If people become better Hindus, better Muslims, better Buddhists by our acts of love, then there is something else growing there." [On another occasion, she again demonstrated her false gospel that 'there are many ways to God': "All is God--Buddhists, Hindus, Christians, etc., all have access to the same God."]

"Calvinism" the Trojan Horse

It should be clear that "Mother" Teresa is anything but an Evangelical Christian. She is a self-sacrificing woman who is following a false religion. Consider some quotes from her speech at the 10/84 Worldwide Retreat for Priests:(a) "At the word of a priest, that little piece of bread becomes the body of Christ, the Bread of Life."(b) "Without a priest, without Jesus going with them, our sisters couldn't go anywhere."(c) "When the priest is there, then can we have our altar and our tabernacle and our Jesus. Only the priest put Jesus there for us. ... Jesus wants to go there, but we cannot bring him unless you first give him to us. This is why I love priests so much. We could never be what we are and do the things we do without you priests who first bring Jesus to us."(d) "Mary ... is our patroness and our Mother, and she is always leading us to Jesus

Calvinism brings not a "good news gospel" but rather "bad news for those not elected! The scriptures teach there is "Rejoicing in the presence of angels over one sinner that repents," Luke 15:10, so if God has already determined by name who will be saved and who will be lost, it will bring no joy to those saints in heaven over their loved ones salvation! If Calvin were correct then when one gets to heaven there can be no fear that a loved one will go to hell or not, since either he was elect or not, and has no choice in whether God "elected" him or not!

Also that would mean no matter how wicked that sinner is, he can have no fear of going to hell since, if he is of the "elect", he cannot be lost, or even be honestly warned to repent lest he go to hell. A warning, as already pointed out, shows a possibility of escaping potential damnation, and, according to Calvinism, there can be no honest "warning" since some will be forced to be saved, and others forced to be damned eternally and the sinner has absolutely no influence with God in regards to his salvation or damnation. Thus more of Calvin's heresy exposed.

When this author was in theological school in Springfield, Mo, the elderly Dr. Peter Connolley, no doubt a Calvinist, made the following statement, "....Why if Jesus did die for the sins of all people, then any lost person on the day of judgment could lay claim to Jesus' death on the cross and not be sent to hell." His comment clearly shows Calvinists confuse "Availability" with "Application". Yes indeed Jesus did die for the sins of all persons, but only those who avail themselves to his free salvation will be saved. "For whosoever shall call upon the name of the Lord shall be saved." (Romans 10:13). A simple illustration as follows shows this precious truth. If this author had a miracle bottle of medicine, which would cure any man of any ailment or disease, only those who would respond to partake of it would be healed, while the rest would suffer. So the medicine is available to all, but only applicable to those who seek it.

A final note: The Word of God has hundreds of warnings, time after time, for the wicked/unsaved to repent and be saved, or suffer the pain of eternal hell. Calvinism unwittingly infers that no unsaved person who is one of the elect, no matter how wicked that person is, needs to worry about the possibility of being sent to hell. According to Calvinism, no one has to be concerned about going to hell since the unsaved wicked, if they have been elected, cannot possibly go to hell so it makes no sense according to Calvinism to warn them...... and of course if not elect then they need not be warned about the terrors of hell and judgment of God in the after life since they are "reprobated" to go to hell anyway with no hope of salvation or repentance. If Calvinism was true, then God would be asking us to preach a lie to warn the unsaved about the possibility of going to hell forever.

"Calvinism" the Trojan Horse

Would God use a lie of impending damnation to those who cannot possibly go there? I think not, but evidently Calvinists do!

Thus why, according to Calvinism, warn any one about hell? Before the appearing of Jesus, John the Baptist testifies to the multitudes about repenting and turning to Jesus Christ. As He warned them strongly that He was not the Messiah but there was one coming, that had the power to forgive sins and He, Jesus Christ would not just baptize with water but would baptize with the Holy Ghost (John 1:33). John the Baptist warned the people, <u>ALL</u> the people that He was just the forerunner and told them what they needed to do to be saved. John did not preach just to the so called "elect", he came as a witness, to bear witness of the Light, which was Christ, that <u>ALL</u> men through him might believe (John 1:7).

Certainly Jesus warned the wicked Pharisees about hell,. "ye generation of vipers, how shall you escape the damnation of hell?" Lk.3:7. Here He plainly tells them that they and they alone were responsible for their impending damnation, not that they were going to hell because God didn't sovereignly elect them! Is it any wonder that Calvinism breeds cold, dead, anti-evangelistic services, and as well relieves Christians of the responsibility of having a working burden for lost souls. Also noteworthy is that very very few Calvinist pastors are able to start and build their own church, but must rely on deceitfully gaining control of an established non-Calvinist evangelical church and slowly change it to their persuasion, which they inevitably will do. Certainly there are many "reformed Calvinistic" churches, openly so, and they do have a right to exist under freedom of religion, but sadly many "non Calvinistic" churches are being slowly infiltrated and taken over by Calvinist preachers and teachers. This needs to be stopped.

CHAPTER FIVE
Calvin's Strange Pernicious Theology

It is well to show to the uninformed, a few of the anti-Biblical teachings Calvin held, and of course when one piously calls himself a "Calvinist" then it is only natural to assume (right or wrong) that he holds to all the same views! (Drawn from Calvin's book... "Institutes of the Christian Religion").

1. Calvin held that God does not offer salvation to all mankind. Book III:21:1.

2. Calvin held that those who differed with him on "sovereignty (and His good pleasure) only for the basis of election to salvation" (such as we who reject unconditional election) are "wicked and blasphemers". (I guess D.L. Moody and Billy Sunday etc. were "wicked and blasphemers"?) Book III:21:1-4.

3. Calvin calls those who oppose his theology "false apostles".(D.L.Moody a false apostle?) Book III21:4.

4. Calvin taught that God chose people to be saved solely by "pleasure" (and of course sovereignty) and nothing else.....thus making those reprobated to eternal hell

going there solely by God's pleasure. Book III 22:1-2.

5. Calvin believed God is a "Just Judge" who damns people he reprobates to eternal hell and saves whom He will according to His goodness. (?) Book III:23:2

6. Calvin taught non-elect babies are condemned to hell by Adam's sin. Ch.23:book3:7

7. Calvin taught that if a person finds he is damned, he must just accept it, and taught that the wicked do use this (being thus cursed) as a license to sin Ch:book3:7

8. Calvin taught that his system of theology was a "secret of God" and that upon persecution by those opposing it that his followers were to keep it a secret. Book III ch.22:9.

9. Calvin taught that "regeneration" is a "renewal of the "Divine image of God" within man. Book III:17:5.

10. Calvin taught only the "elect" were called to be saved. 23:13

11. Calvin taught that those lost who accept his system of theology, and then use it as a license to sin (naturally what else would they do if they are "reprobated to hell"), are "filthy swine". Ch. 23:12.

12. Calvin admits his brand of theology "breeds" lawlessness. 23:12

13. Calvin says God raises up reprobates in order that His glory may be displayed. Book III:22:11

14. Calvin taught that not all men were "created equal". Quoting as follows… "By Predestination we mean the

eternal decree of God by which he determined with himself whatever He wanted to happen with regard to every man. All are not created on equal terms but some are preordained to eternal life, others to eternal damnation, and accordingly as such have been created for one or other of these ends, we say that he has been predestinated to life or to death." Book III:25:3.

15. Calvin taught that those opposing infant baptism are "reprobate spirits influenced by Satan". Ch.16:4,31-32. (Calvin holding Lutzer as a reprobate spirit? *Lutzer holds to believers baptism only and still considers Calvin a great man of God? ed.)*

16. Calvin taught that elect/chosen infants are regenerated (and receive forgiveness of sins. Book 4:22) at baptism and are then engrafted in to the body of Christ. Book 4, ch.14:22-23.

17. Calvin wrongly equates "pre-science (or pre-knowledge or foreknowledge) with "divine appointment". Book III ch.23:6-7.

18. Calvin teaches God does not elect according to man's choice of Him *(as is really the Truth ed.)*, but rather by His (God's) goodness and pleasure. Ch.23:10.

Reader Note: Certainly, and sadly, IT can be said that the Calvinist Jesus surely endorses some abortions! How so one may ask? simple. If all babies are either of the elect or of the non elec as calvinism teaches, then those aborted who are of the non elect, are quickly ushered out of this life and into hell fire, rather than to be allowed to grow up as unsaved, non elect reprobates corrupting others and breeding more sin and lawlessness. how could abortion of the non elect be a sin or a crime against god since the earth is thereby rid or purged of one more corrupting human life, a life which will end anyway with it's entrance into hellfire for eternity? Here it is that all calvinists unwittingly endorse the murder of innocent babies provided they are of the non elect. This author can surely hear some calvinist couple entertain aborting their unborn child due a difficult pregnancy etc, since god (supposedly) ORDAINS all things that come to pass. thus if they do elect to abortion, it certainly was due to god ordianing it since it happened, and that the embryo must therefore have been a non elect embryo. think also of the fact that maybe 50-70%(?) of the world is not christian, especially not of the evangelical type. That being the case, then that large percentage (according to Calvinism) not being of the "elect" could justifiably be aborted, so why not legalize the same? so, How could aborting a non elect reprobate who is going to spend eternity in hell anyway be a crime or a sin against God? Perhaps a Calvinist could argue if a non elect embryo is aborted by mistake, well they go to heaven anyway. as previously seen in this paper, According to calvin god 'hates' non elect babies since they are supposedly born guilty sinners, so why not abort them? herein lies calvinist convoluted thinking and inferences! No matter what calvinism may believe or teach abortion is murder!

Also note: Calvin falsely held INFANTS are TOTALLY depraved sinners, but if so, is this (Matt.19:14 suffer the little children to come unto me for of such is the Kingdom of God) Kingdom God builds, built on totally depraved sinners or ratheron purity and innocence as personified by precious innocent children and infants which contradicts Calvins own doctrine?!

JOHN CALVIN'S GOSPEL
VS.
THE GOSPEL OF THE WORD OF GOD

Calvin's gospel, the false gospel of unconditional election or forced/fatalistic salvation for only a few, is in direct contradiction with the Gospel jesus Christ died and paid for with his precious blood, the gospel of the word of God which plainly teaches the availablity of salvation for all men, everywhere of all nations.

Calvin's Strange Pernicious Theology

Calvinists and Calvinist sympathizers need to be but reminded of Uzzah in II Sam.6:6, when David was moving the ark of God and as the oxen shook the ark and Uzzah put forth his hand to steady it, the Lord smote him dead. Now how dare the Calvinists seek to supplant the Gospel of the Bible with the false gospel of Calvinism and unconditional election! How holy and sacred is the precious Gospel of free salvation offered to all men, and paid for with the sinless spotless blood of Jesus Christ! Sad indeed is the fact that so many of the "upper echelon" of the evangelical circles, pastors, teachers, evangelists etc, ignorantly hold to Calvin's heresies, and go on and on unchallenged.

Is it not outrageous to believe and teach (as Calvinists do) that God has decreed and ordained all things etc. that take place including "intending for man to sin," and then see the many many times in scripture where God pours out His wrath upon wicked men and nations who practice and do these wicked things, (things which He supposedly decreed and intended them to do!). Then also, He supposedly sends the majority of humanity to burn in fire and brimstone in the lake of fire for eternity for doing what He ordained and decreed them to do! Outrageous! No, the scripture is plain, if man does go to hell, it is because he refused God's plan of salvation entirely on his own. Calvinists (using mental gymnastics) play upon the words "Certainty" and "Necessity," saying they are two different terms, that God's decrees cause "Certainty" but not the "Necessity" for man to sin, thus supposedly theologically freeing Him from being involved as partners in the sinfulness of man.

See web site "corkfpc.com/shedd.html" to further explore these heresies. One last point here, Calvinists need to answer the following. "Why would God command, "Acts 17:30: But now God commands all men everywhere to repent" if not all men can repent, and if not all men can be saved as they falsely claim! A perfect example showing that ALL men could and could have been saved, and not just the "frozen chosen."

Calvinists make much use of the term "sovereign grace" to denote their basic doctrinal position. This is a very subtle attempt to water down their fatalistic doctrines to be more palatable to non-Calvinists. When in college this author would be challenged by Calvinists with the statement, "Why we merely believe in the sovereign grace of God in providing salvation, you believe that do you not?" To which of course I would agree that I did, but that I did not (and still don't) see the Word of God as teaching that men are forced to be saved or damned as they teach. Sovereign grace certainly is a doctrine of scripture but it does not mean what they teach it means. Also this author believes the churches have been wrongly influenced away from being very pointed in their invitations with such statements as "… If you are not saved you can come and be saved tonight," or "… If you want to be saved come forward during the invitation," to such statements as " Come and trust Jesus as your Savior," or receive Jesus tonight." Admittedly while these latter statements are scriptural they are a move away from very pointed and effective invitation giving.

HARD TEST FOR SKEPTICS

Sad so many well-known pastors, evangelists, and teachers, while not Calvinists, are unwitting sympathizers with those who are. They refuse to break fellowship with them and simply look upon Calvinism as "Just another harmless theological opinion." So, following is a self test for these "limp wrist" sympathizers….

Choose the correct answer from the following (i.e. Which is the biblical gospel plan of salvation?)

The test as follows: Jesus' sacrificial death was sufficient for all but:

A.   He died only for the Jews.

B.   He died only for Christians and Jews.

C.   He died only for the white race.

D.   He died only for the black race.

E.   He died only for some excluding all others from possibiblity of salvation.(Calvinism)

F.   He died for all to the exclusion of none providing the possibility for all people of all ages to be saved

(For the first 400 years of church history so called double predestination was totally unheard of!).

Now all of the above represent a different plan of salvation, but only "F" can be correct according to the Word of God. Only "F" can scripturally fulfill the wonderful gospel plan of salvation thus excluding all the others. Praise the Lord for Jn.3:16. Notice also, Titus 2:11-12, "For the grace of God that bringeth salvation hath appeared to **ALL** men…"

JESUS DIED ONLY FOR NON-CALVINISTS SO CALVINISTS CANNOT BE SAVED!

Yes this above statement is indeed false and outrageous and no doubt would enrage Calvinists if preached as true…but then they provide the same outrage to unsaved persons by teaching that not all unsaved are/nor can be candidates for eternal salvation! Calvinists hide behind the doctrine of the sovereignty of God believing they are giving exaltation and glory to God by saying "God does what he chooses and we should not question it," when their false doctrine of double (forced) predestination raises the anger of non Calvinists.

"Calvinism" the Trojan Horse

Calvinism is certainly a false gospel and needs to be repudiated and renounced! It is of interest that many who hold to the doctrines of Calvin, do not call themselves Calvinists since the same doctrines were preached and taught much earlier by Augustine, the Ana-Baptist etc.

Also since non-Calvinists hold to "general provision of the Atonement or that the Atonement is available to ALL men, Calvinists call these persons "Armenians" believing that there is only one option to the T.U.L.I.P....i.e Armenianism. (As far as this author knows most if not all Armenians do not hold to the eternal security of the believer.)

It is this authors firm belief that no person, upon conversion, simply reading the Word of God can come to the conclusion of "double predestination" or "forced salvation and forced damnation". Yes they must be "spoon fed" that terrible doctrine by followers of Calvin. Following is a perfect example of how Calvinists desecrate precious hymns of the faith which also include "Just As I Am"...... "Come Every Soul By Sin Oppressed"....etc.

Rev. J. L. of Elgin, S.C., in debating a Calvinist on line, wrote me that he received the following during a debate: He wrote as follows:

Terry,

I posted this thought from your notes (along with the lyrics to the song) to some other preachers. One Reformed Presbyterian answered thusly:

J. L. wrote:

Sad indeed, no Calvinist can honestly sing "Rescue the Perishing" since according to them,

(A) the elect need not be rescued since they are in no danger of eternal damnation, and (B) the non-elect cannot be saved anyway so no need to seek to rescue them!

Rescue the Perishing (Words by Fanny J. Crosby)
Verse 1
Rescue the perishing; care for the dying.
Snatch them in pity from sin and the grave.
Weep o'er the erring one; lift up the fallen.
Tell them of Jesus, the mighty to save.

Chorus:
Rescue the perishing; care for the dying. Jesus is merciful; Jesus will save!

Verse 2
Tho' they are slighting Him, still He is waiting:
Waiting the penitent child to receive.
Plead with them earnestly; plead with them gently.
He will forgive if they only believe.

Verse 3
Down in the human heart, crushed by the tempter,
Feelings lie buried that grace can restore.
Touched by a loving heart, wakened by kindness,
Cords that are broken will vibrate once more.

Verse 4
Rescue the perishing; duty demands it.
Strength for your labor the Lord will provide.
Back to the narrow way patiently win them,
Tell the poor wanderer a Savior has died.

(The reformed Calvinist Presbyterian pastor answered as follows. Ed.)
J.L.,

> Aside from your mischaracterizations of Reformed thought I certainly wouldn't sing this song anyway - It is theologically and biblically inaccurate. Man can't even save and rescue himself let alone someone else. Salvation belongs to the Lord. He is the one who rescues. He may use someone else or myself to bring the message of the Gospel, but I do not save/rescue anyone. This song is very man-centered. I say cast it in the garbage can where it belongs.
>
> Peace, Steve

No doubt, Calvin would readily class Fannie Crosby who wrote so many precious, sacred hymns as a "wicked, blaspheming, false prophetess" since her hymns do not do his theology justice. Certainly she was not a Calvinist, thank the Lord. (See "2-3" under "Calvin's pernicious theology" above.) Calvinists no doubt hate the beautiful and cherished Christmas song "Joy to the World" as well. "Joy to the world the Lord is come, let earth receive her King…let every heart prepare Him room….." Here is a song that proclaims salvation is meant for "all" people, and that "all" are candidates for salvation! This is only one of many more songs Calvinists must hate and hold in disrepute due to their perverted theology.

DEBATE CALVINISTS?

This author doubts such efforts are effective in reaching Calvinists except to perhaps enlighten Christians who are ignorant of Calvinism by such debates. There are only two responses to confronting a rattlesnake, destroy it or shun it and run! The same with Calvinistic doctrine and their wresting of Holy Scripture. Surely the Calvinist translation of Jn. 3:16 would be as follows:

> For God so loved those he sovereignly elected, that He gave His only Begotten Son to die for them and them alone, that when whosoever of those elect believed on Him, because He caused them to believe, then they the elect, shall not perish but have everlasting life.

CHAPTER SIX
Final Thoughts on Augustinian / Calvinism

Calvinists are quick to point out that "As in Adam all die" (Rom.5), so all those dead in trespasses and sins must be elected according to Gods sovereign election. What Calvinists are forgetting is as follows:

1. Immediately after Adam sinned and thus died "in that day thou shalt surely die..." i.e. immediately though he "died spiritually he was still: a. Conscious. b. Able to communicate/negotiate with God when God confronted him for his disobedience. c. Was able to voluntarily avail himself to the sacrificial benefits of the slain animal and the covering of skins as an atonement. (Thus to say as the Calvinists say, that all unsaved men are "dead to God" which supposedly means totally insensitive and unable to communicate his need of Salvation to God, totally falls apart. "Dead" in the Biblical sense means "separation" from God not "insensitive to God".)

2. Thus Calvinists place the entire human race under condemnation, consigned for eternal hell by Adams

sin being imputed to all of humanity unless God sovereignly elects some to be saved.

3. But here is where they forget that Adam did not have one choice, but rather TWO choices! Certainly if his first choice to sin automatically damned the entire human race which proceeded from his loins and God accepted that choice for all as Romans 5 indicates, then his second choice to be saved (and I don't know any theologian that believes Adam went to hell) was certainly honored by God to offer to the entire human race the possibility of eternal salvation for all! Clearly the term "many" in Rom.5:15 means "all", or the unknown large number of persons ever born since all die in Adam, and therefore the "many" for whom Christ died referring as well to "all". If all sin in Adam and are damned, then in Adam's second choice also all are offered the possibility of free salvation and eternal life. Nothing indicating in the scripture here that God does not offer salvation to all as they falsely teach. (And no… God does not tell us to offer salvation to all since one does not know who are the elect and who are not as they falsely teach…No….God does not ask us to give a false invitation to all men, but an honest invitation to ALL since ALL can come be saved!.) Jesus told his disciples to go into the hedges and highways and compel ALL to come in!

Final Thoughts on Augustinian / Calvinism

SPURGEON AND CALVINISM

"I have my own private opinion that there is no such thing as preaching Christ and Him crucified, unless we preach what nowadays is called Calvinism. It is a nickname to call it Calvinism; Calvinism is the gospel, and nothing else. I do not believe we can preach the gospel, if we do not preach justification by faith, without works; nor unless we preach the sovereignty of God in His dispensation of grace; nor unless we exalt the electing, unchangeable, eternal, immutable, conquering love of Jehovah; nor do I think we can preach the gospel, unless we base it upon the special and particular redemption of His elect and chosen people which Christ wrought out upon the cross; nor can I comprehend a gospel which lets saints fall away after they are called, and suffers the children of God to be burned in the fires of damnation after having once believed in Jesus. Such a gospel I abhor." (Quotation of Spurgeon from reformed.com).

Interesting to note that Calvinists proudly point to Spurgeon (who was known as the "Prince of Preachers") for his endorsement of Calvinistic theology as stated above. This author sees it a little differently. While he did indeed state this endorsement, the bold italics shows this was his private (not public) opinion, and his emphasis was not on the "frozen chosen" but rather on *basic* scriptural trues which contradict Armenianism as a whole. It is this authors opinion that many many people hold/held doctrines of Calvin (including Spurgeon) without seriously thinking thru the contradictory conclusions that one must be come to when embracing the same in the light of Holy Scripture. Certainly the end inferences of Calvinism are preposterous. To Spurgeon's credit he certainly was evangelistic, and had a deep love in his heart for winning the lost and as well held the sinner's full responsibility to repent and be saved and as well believed that all could be saved! (That alone proves he did not fully ascribe to Calvinism, since no true Calvinist believes that all men could be saved). If Calvinists had as great a love for lost souls as Spurgeon and did as much as he did in winning them to Christ who could fault them except in their theological beliefs?

Following is an interesting take on Spurgeon and his belief on Calvinism: From: "jesus-is-savior.com".

The Truth of the Matter

I believe that Calvin misunderstood the Bible, and Spurgeon misunderstood Calvin. Yes, it is true that a person cannot be saved unless God the Holy Spirit is working in their heart, but the Bible plainly teaches that it's the Holy Spirit's task to convict THE WORLD of sin, righteousness, and judgment. Yes, God knew in advance (before the world began) who would one day trust Him, and He predestinated them to be conformed TO THE IMAGE OF HIS SON, but NOT to salvation. God NEVER chooses anyone to be saved. He did predestinate them before the world began, but only because He saw that those people would one day choose of their own free will to be saved. God NEVER forces anyone to be saved, nor does God ever choose anyone to be saved. *(Further he states)* John Calvin taught heresy when he taught that God chooses people to be saved. There is NOT one Scripture in the entire Word of God which teaches that God chooses anyone to be saved. The Bible teaches that all believers were predestined to "be conformed to the image of His Son," NOT predestined to salvation ("For whom he did foreknow, he also did predestinate to be conformed to the image of his Son, that he might be the firstborn among many brethren" -Romans 8:29). This is exactly what Spurgeon believed. In contrast, Calvinism DOES teach predestination unto salvation. God NEVER chooses anyone for salvation; Scriptures such as Acts 17:30 make this abundantly clear ("...but now commandeth all men every where to repent"). Why would God command ALL men to repent if only certain men have been chosen for salvation. *(And further)* It is apparent that Spurgeon was only a one-point Calvinist. Spurgeon believed that "whosoever will" can come to Christ to be saved. This eliminates three points of Calvinism. Spurgeon also believed in eternal security, which eliminates the last point of Calvinism. The only Calvinist heresy that Spurgeon bought into, and horribly so, was the unbiblical heresy of limited atonement. Clearly, Christ died and shed His blood for ALL humanity. (End of quote.)

A BLUNDERING CREATOR?

The Word of God directly contradicts the following premise of Calvin, " ... Not all men are created with a similar destiny but eternal life is foreordained for some, and eternal damnation for others. Every man, therefore, being created for one or the other of these ends, we say, is predestined either to life or to death." So boasts Calvin.

Taking this false premise which is never stated in the Word of God, and taking the following Biblical statement of Pink (a noted very strong Calvinist) clearly shows the Calvinists unwittingly create an idea that God was indeed a "blundering Creator, insulting and degrading His own creation."

PINK STATES AS FOLLOWS:

God has not left us in ignorance of how He regards those who have openly and persistently defied Him. Again and again the Bible makes known to us the solemn fact that God looks upon the wicked as cumberers of the earth, as repugnant to Him. They are represented as "dross" not gold (Psalm 119:119); as worthless "chaff (Matthew 3:12); as "vipers" (Matthew 12:34); as "vessels unto dishonor" and "vessels of wrath" (Romans 9:21, 22); as those who are to be made the Lord's footstool (1 Corinthians 15:2 7) as "trees whose fruit withereth, without fruit, twice dead, plucked up by the roots" (Jude 12) and therefore fit for nothing but the fire; as those who will be "spued out of the Lord's mouth" (Revelation 3:16), that is, as objects of revulsion. Some of these passages describe Jewish reprobates, others sinners of the Gentiles; some refer to those who lived in a bygone dispensation, others belong to the present; some speak of men this side of the grave, some of those on the other side. One purpose in calling attention to them is to show how God regards his enemies. The estimate expressed in the above passages (and they might easily be multiplied) cannot be harmonized with the view that God still looks upon them in love and entertains only the most tender regards for them.

Another class of passages may be referred to in this connection.

> "For I lift up My hand to heaven, and say, I live forever. If I whet My glittering sword, and Mine hand take hold on judgment; I will render vengeance to Mine enemies, and will reward them that hate Me. I will make Mine arrows drunk with blood, and my sword shall devour flesh; and that with the blood of the slain and of the captives, from the beginning of revenges upon the enemy" (Deuteronomy 32:40-42).

Can this be made to square with the theory that God has naught but compassion toward those who have despised and defied Him?

Final Thoughts on Augustinian / Calvinism

> "Because I have called, and ye have refused; I have stretched out My hand, and no man regarded; But ye have set at nought all My counsel, and would none of My reproof; I also will laugh at your calamity; I will mock when your fear cometh; When your fear cometh as desolation, and your destruction cometh as a whirlwind; when distress and anguish cometh upon you. Then shall they call upon Me, but I will not answer; they shall seek Me early, but they shall not find Me" (Proverbs 1:24-28).

Is this the language of One who still has designs of mercy toward His enemies?

> "I have trodden the winepress alone; and of the people there was none with Me; for I will tread them in Mine anger, and trample them in My fury; and their blood shall be sprinkled upon My garments, and I will stain all My raiment" (Isaiah 63:3).

Weigh this carefully, and then ask if such treatment is meted out toward those unto whom the Lord cherishes nought but compassion.

Should it be said, Each of these passages is from the Old Testament, it would be sufficient to say, True, but it is the same God as the New Testament reveals that is there speaking. But consider one verse from the New Testament also. The Christ of God is yet going to say to men,

> "Depart from Me, ye cursed into everlasting fire" (Matthew 25:41). (End of Pink quote from Reformed.org).

Now suppose an inventor were to mass produce an automobile engine which had failure deliberately designed into it, and then when

"Calvinism" the Trojan Horse

they began to fail the inventor becomes outraged at their failure and decides to recall and correctly rebuild a small number of engines without those weaknesses. He then recalls the others (the majority) to be scrapped and permanently destroyed. Now that is the idiocy of Calvinism! God is supposed to be a Creator who designed and created mankind with potentially inherent failure/weakness in him. Then since He foresaw that all would fail and sin against Him, He sovereignly (?) selects/elects certain few to be regenerated and saved, while He in outrage against the wickedness of the rest condemns them, the majority, to burn in torment in an everlasting hell/lake of fire!

The above quotation from Pink (which does correctly portray the Lords anger against the wicked) coupled with Calvinism, paints such a Creator, one whose creation reflects his absolute sovereignty, and then He pours out His wrath and anger on those whom He neglects or refuses to elect unto salvation and eventual perfection in Christ. Certainly a picture of a dufuss blundering Creator. What an insult to the Almighty! What evil heresy, and to think that many non Calvinist colleges etc, allow Calvinists to freely teach and preach from their pulpits or to have small numbers of them to group and fellowship in their midst! The only way anyone can come to embrace the doctrines of Calvinism is for someone to teach them the Bible in the light *(sorry, "in the darkness" ed.)* of Calvinistic doctrines, now that is a fact.

To preach two opposing gospels to the world is what amounts to preaching the fatalism of Calvinism vs. the biblical gospel of free salvation available to all. When Calvinism is preached, it must be remembered that the hearers are unsaved needing to be evangelized. Those hearers have natural intelligence and are able to respond to a choice. Take for instance a wicked depraved reprobated sinner such as was Count Sade De Marquis. This man was perhaps histories most depraved, corrupt kidnapper, pedophile, murderer/rapists ever to live. His crimes against humanity are absolutely without equal in this authors (and others) opinion. Now according to Calvinism, were he to hear and accept the doctrines of Calvin, this man would no doubt come to the following conclusion. "Well, if it is true that I am one of the secretly elect and will one day be saved, then I shall continue in my depravity since I am in no danger of going to hell. If I am not one of the secretly elect, then I am in no danger of going to hell since I have no possibility of being saved anyway. Therefore I may as well continue in my pleasures of depravity. Either way it is God's decision if I am saved or not, not mine." On the other hand, if he were to be exposed to the Biblical plan of salvation, that salvation is open to all then he would naturally reason as follows. "I am a wicked sinner, I know, so since salvation is open to me no doubt, if I do not repent and accept Christ for deliverance from sin and hell, it is totally my fault if I go to hell for eternity." Here it is clearly seen why even in Calvin's mind that Calvinist theology "breeds lawlessness." See 11-12 under "Calvin's Pernicious Theology" chapter 5.

THE BLESSEDNESS OF PERSONAL SOUL WINNING

Calvinists can never enjoy soul winning as they should since their theology rejects the idea of "Rescue the Perishing" as stated earlier. Years ago, this author, driven with (and thankfully still driven with) the burden that souls will go to hell if we do not faithfully witness (which no Calvinist believes) and attempt to win souls to Christ, had the wonderful experience as follows: One summer day going door to door alone to win the lost, I came to a duplex with a man sitting on one side in a rocking chair.

"Calvinism" the Trojan Horse

The man perhaps 40-50 years old, sat silently as I went to the other door, knocked and left tracts in the door since no one was home. Then as I approached him, and attempted to talk to him, he said "I am not interested and don't need any." Now here a Calvinist would give up believing the man was not prompted by the Holy Spirit to reveal if he was one of the "elect" or not. I answered that "I am not trying to get you to come to any church or change churches, I merely want to take a few minutes to explain to you how you can be sure you are going to heaven or not when you die."

Immediately his attitude changed, and he said "OK, I'm alright with that," so I proceeded to take him through the plan of salvation Finally at the end, I asked him if he wanted to be saved and he said yes, so I led him in the sinner's prayer. While he was praying after me, about half way through the prayer, I heard a strange high pitch groan as he exhaled deeply, to which of course I ignored and finished the prayer with him praying behind me till the end.

After the prayer, I asked him if he got saved during the prayer, to which he paused for some brief time and said, "I just got out of the hospital, the doctor said I have terminal cancer and am going to die shortly.... he sent me home to die. Did you hear that groan I made during prayer? That was the first decent breath of air I have ever had in my life, yes I am saved!" Yes, we both had tears in our eyes! A Calvinist cannot "rescue the perishing" nor be concerned that precious souls will die and go to hell if they are not witnessed to, thus the gutted gospel of Calvinism. Calvinism will destroy the motivation of the soul winner! Flee it!

Reader Note: Interesting note. This week, June 4, 10, on his "running to win" radio broadcast, five point calvinsit Dr. Lutzer stated in essence concerning false prophets/teachers; let us learn to identify the earmarks of false teachers/prophets and LET US run with it!

HYPER-CALVINISM DEFINED

It is plain in studying the heresies of Calvinism that ALL Calvinists, that is the so called "Hyper-Calvinists, **and** the regular Calvinists" are no different from one the other except in their approach to evangelism, and they all believe and adhere to "another gospel." Most Calvinists descreetly hide behind the attitude, "Well I am certainly not a Hyper-Calvinist even though we all believe in the doctrines of grace. The Hyper-Calvinists have a different view on evangelism which we regular Calvinists do not hold!"

So what, then, is a hyper-Calvinist? (Quoting from a regular Calvinist at, "challies.com/arch"). "Part of the confusion about this term no doubt arises from the use of the prefix "hyper." "Hyper" does not refer, as many might think, to enthusiasm or excitement. Rather its basic meaning is along the lines of "excessive or excessively." You might think of the word hyperactive which means "excessively active." Hyper- comes from the Greek prefix huper-, which comes from the preposition huper, meaning "over, beyond." So a hyper-Calvinist is one who goes beyond and over the bounds of what Calvinism teaches (and thus over the bounds of what the Bible teaches). He is excessive in his application of the doctrines. This manifests itself in an over-emphasis of one aspect of God's character at the expense of another. Hyper-Calvinists emphasize God's sovereignty but de-emphasize God's love. They tend to set God's sovereignty at odds with the clear biblical call to human responsibility. We can see how these are worked out as we look at a concise definition of the term. Phil Johnson, who has done extensive research on this subject very helpfully defines hyper-Calvinists using a five-fold definition. A hyper-Calvinist is one who:

1. Denies that the gospel call applies to all who hear, OR
2. Denies that faith is the duty of every sinner, OR
3. Denies that the gospel makes any "offer" of Christ, salvation, or mercy to the non- elect (or denies that the offer of divine mercy is free and universal),) OR
4. Denies that there is such a thing as "common grace," OR
5. Denies that God has any sort of love for the non-elect.

As Phil says, "All five varieties of hyper-Calvinism undermine evangelism or twist the gospel message." So this is the key to understanding hyper-Calvinism: it undermines evangelism and/or somehow distorts the gospel message.

Probably the most distinguishing characteristic of a Hyper-Calvinist is an unwillingness to evangelize at all, or to evangelize without extending a call to accept and believe the gospel. An example of a hyper-Calvinistic confession makes this clear. Article 33 of *Articles of Faith of the Gospel Standard Aid and Poor Relief Societies* says, "Therefore, that for ministers in the present day to address unconverted persons, or indiscriminately all in a mixed congregation, calling upon them to savingly repent, believe, and receive Christ, or perform any other acts dependent upon the new creative power of the Holy Ghost, is, on the one hand, to imply creature power, and on the other, to deny the doctrine of special redemption." In other words, they say, to command people to turn from their sin and to repent is to command them to do something they are unable to do for this would deny the doctrine of particular redemption. Yet this teaching is clearly at odds with the Bible's call for all men to believe. The offer of the gospel is universal and God truly does command all men to

Final Thoughts on Augustinian / Calvinism

heed it. Faith is a duty for all men. God's common grace extends to all men and, while God does not love elect and non-elect in the same way, the Bible is clear that He does love all that He has created.

Keep that five-fold definition in mind and you'll have a good idea of what it truly means to be a hyper-Calvinist. Of course I have little confidence that articles like this one will make any real difference. The term hyper-Calvinist is a convenient and baggage-filled one to lob into an argument or discussion. But at least now we know whether or not we truly fit that mold!" (End of quote by a regular Calvinist).

Now here is something shocking indeed! When re-reading these "5" points about what a hyper-Calvinist is defined as by "regular Calvinist" Phil Johnson, it becomes clear that any one who calls himself a "Calvinist" then can be defined as a hyper-Calvinist! The simple reason being that all Calvinists believe in "unconditional election" or "particular redemption." So....

1. How can the gospel call apply to "all" who hear it preached if only the elect can be saved?
2. How can faith be the duty of every sinner if some cannot be saved?
3. How can God honestly offer salvation to the non-elect if they cannot be saved?
4. How can God extend "common grace" to all if some cannot be saved?
5. How can God have any love for those He has supposedly chosen as "vessels of wrath" or as "reprobates?"

Another interesting point is that the above quote from "challies.com/arch" which says, "So a hyper-Calvinist is one who goes beyond and over the bounds of what Calvinism teaches (and thus over the bounds of what the Bible teaches)." What he needs to wake up and realize is that the afore "five" points of what a "hyper-Calvinist" is according to him, actually falls easily into the framework of what Calvin taught! That cannot be disputed! To claim differently is dishonest!

Final Thoughts on Augustinian / Calvinism

"THE NON-ELECT JUDGED" EXPLANATION THEREOF FOLLOWING

No doubt this cartoon is inflammatory to say the least, BUT, that it clearly portrays the heretical views of Calvin is irrefutable. Jesus plainly taught, "Suffer the little children to come unto me for of such is the kingdom of God." Calvin taught that "some" little children/babies could not come to Jesus since they were not of the elect. Jesus did not use the term "some" to qualify a small minority of babies and small children to be saved! God "hates" non-elect babies? Calvin thinks so as follows:

Calvin's Institutes Book 4, Ch.16:17 Subject: Babies not justified are hated by God.
Quoting Calvin as follows. "In fine, if Christ speaks truly when he declares that he is life, we must necessarily be engrafted into him by whom we are delivered from the bondage of death. But "how?"... they (ed. "they" being the ones opposed to infants being saved or lost according to election) ask, are infants regenerated when not possessing a knowledge of either good or evil? We answer that the work of God, though beyond the reach of our capacity, is not therefore null. Moreover, infants who are to be saved (and that some are saved at this age is certain) must without question be previously regenerated by the Lord. For if they bring innate corruption with them from their mothers womb, they must be purified before they can be admitted in the kingdom of God into which shall not enter anything that defiles (Rev. 21:27).

If they are born sinners as David and Paul affirm, they must either remain unaccepted and hated by God or be justified Author: John Calvin.

Then lastly on the "Decree of God" to consign non elect infants to eternal death (ed. ..hell) Book 3, ch.23:7. Calvin states, "I again ask how is it that the fall of Adam involves so many nations with their infant children in eternal death ("eternal hell" ed.) without remedy, unless that it so seemed meet to God? Here the most loquacious tongues must be dumb. The decree I admit is dreadful and yet it is impossible to deny that God foreknew what the end of man was to be before he made him and foreknew because he had so ordained by his decree. Author: John Calvin.

So who are we to believe, Jesus or Calvin?
Millions and millions of precious souls over the centuries have lived and died having never heard of, or known of that false doctrine of Unconditional Election. So if Calvinism is true then this cartoon will certainly accurately portray the coming judgment!

Conclusion

If Calvinism is left unchecked and unchallenged it will spread through out all of our evangelical institutions and churches bringing deadness and ruin with it. Not only that but once it establishes itself as the "true gospel" those of us who are not Calvinists will be shut out and labeled as those who are preaching "another gospel"! God forbid should this ever happen. The implication of such a false theological system is that "Calvinism is the way the truth and the light" and that "no man cometh to the Father but by the sovereign election at the pleasure of God the Father." The fatalistic false doctrines of Augustinian/Calvinism are indeed evil and slanderous of a loving and compassionate God and as well should be classified as "doctrines of devils." To say, "Well yes he is a Calvinist, but a good man and doing a good work for the Lord," is to speak good of evil. The scripture warns "Woe unto them that speak evil of good, and good of evil." Is.5:20. A final thought: Sad indeed, no Calvinist can honestly sing "Rescue the Perishing" (and many other sacred hymns and songs) since according to them,

(A) the elect need not be rescued since they are in no danger of eternal damnation, and

(B) the non-elect cannot be saved anyway so no need to seek to rescue them!

"Calvinism" the Trojan Horse

Sad also… so many "great Baptist scholars" come and gone have (to some degree) ignorantly given their endorsement to Augustinian/Calvinistic doctrine,

Baptist theologians, such as Abraham Booth, J. P. Boyce, John Bunyan, B. H. Carroll, Alexander Carson, J. L. Dagg, E. C. Dargan, T. T. Eaton, D. F. Estes, D. B. Ford, J. M. Frost, Andrew Fuller, Richard Fuller, John Gill, A. J. Gordon, J. R. Graves, Robert Haldane, Robert Hall, Alvah Hovey, J. B. Moody, E. Y. Mullins, J. M. Pendleton, A. W. Pink, J. W. Porter, W. B. Riley, E. G. Robinson, T. T. Shields, T. P. Simmons, C. H. Spurgeon, A. H. Strong, R. A. Venable.

Only the judgment seat of Christ and eternity will show the damage these doctrines have done.

Another thought: If Calvinism is true, then no one could ever be said to be lost except for the non-elect, and that would void the call to evangelize! Why? Simply because if God did "pre-elect" certain to be saved in eternity past, then that would mean that the elect never were "lost" and were "safe" due to "pre-election." If the non-elect then are the only truly "lost" (the elect being "presaved/safe") then the commanded message of the cross to evangelize them is voided. How can one evangelize the non-elect lost who are irretrievably lost and not truly candidates for salvation? Here again, Calvinism countering our Savior's message to reach the lost, and destroying incentive to "go" and preach the gospel to every creature!

Perhaps it is of no wonder that there are secret societies who secretly worship Satan. Calvinsim, when it is closely examined, places God Jehovah as the real author of sin by "intending for man and Satan to sin." This hideous idea places the Lord and Satan on the same page in the ruination and fall of the entire human race into sin depravity, shame and damnation. Their goals then become identical

Conclusion

for man in his fall and damnation. The only difference is that for some unknown or secret reason God decides to elect some few of those poor damned souls to salvation and send the rest to endless damnation along with the Devil and his angels. If say a man brings up his son and daughter in an environment of drugs, prostitution and immorality with the intention they become involved, then he himself becomes guilty of their sins! To say God intended for man and Satan to sin, makes Him personally responsible for all the sins of mankind and makes Him an unholy God! In such an absurd case, God looses His holiness, ceases being worthy of worship, and then changing His mind, turns on Satan and his angels, as well as the non-elect and casts them to burn in hell forever. Since He sent Jesus the spotless sinless Lamb of God to die for the sins of the 'elect' He would need redemption as well for His fall else the Trinity would be forever alienated from each other. Following Calvinism to its logical (illogical) conclusion teaches just such heresy. Amazing that pastors proudly proclaim they are of the "Reformed (Calvinistic) Theology." The real goal of exposing Calvinism here is not to divide the Church, but rather to root out heresy from the Christian Church bringing all born again believers under one banner... The banner of TRUTH!

Pray that Calvinism will be shown to be for what it really is and thus will be rooted out of our Bible believing churches!

On the day of judgement, who will stand before God and give account of preaching a false Gospel? Those who preach that salvation is available to all of humanity of all nations, or those who preach that salvation is only available to a few whom God soverignly chose, consigning the rest/majority to be tormented in hell fire and the lake of fire for all eternity?!

THE CORRECT VIEW OF PREDESTINATION

Absolutely, God knows the end from the beginning, and the beginning to the end, regarding any and all circumstances that ever possibly will be or could be. To deny such is too refute the foreknowledge and omniscience of Almighty God, and this author knows of no one who would debate that, except an atheist. The fact that our Holy Scriptures, given under Divine inspiration of God, do lay out all future events from Eden to the final new heaven and earth, and have shown to be exactly prophetically correct down to the smallest matter (thus far and so will into the future), proves the Omniscient/foreknowledge of God.

The Calvinist says (in error) that such shows that God controls and causes all events to transpire according to His perfect will, so the end will come out as He sees fit. Such a view, as this booklet explains, makes God the author of sin with Satan as His accomplice. Such cannot be, so that premise falls along with Calvinism. God cannot sin, nor is He the author of sin! On the other hand, the other view is simply that as we live our lives, in accordance with our free will actions, what we as humanity choose to do, simply determines what God foresaw as He in His omniscience read the future of man from a beginning point in eternity past. Thus in eternity past, while He foreseeing all coming events, interjected His will into whatever events necessary, that the outcome would be in accordance with His will. At that point, the future was permanently locked.

Thus it comes down to, what you and I choose to do, determines what God foreknew would take place, and thus locks our future in place as we live our lives out, (with of course God intervening where and how He pleases). So, the simplest way to define God's predestination is, "What we choose to do as we live our lives, determines God's foreknowledge in eternity past. Last thought. What about Satan, why cannot he be curbed and begin to be benevolent/caring/ and truly helpful to mankind, as we humans can become when we are born again? Possibly simple answer is that what God foresaw the future actions of Satan being up until his judgment in the Lake of Fire, were only outside of His will, and so thus his wickedness was irretrievably locked in stone.

MISCELANOUS CONTEMPORARY ISSUES AFFLICTING AND ATTACKING BIBLICAL CHRISTIANITY

Sadly, the evangelical church today is assaulted with so many heresies, besides John Calvin's "other gospel of forced salvation and forced damnation" (Calvinists generally are NOT strong personal soul winners but with rare exceptions, nor ever can be since they operate under his fatalistic doctrine.) Calvinism…The gospel of the evil one to lure Christians away from urgently spreading the gospel, making them shrug off the need of urgency to try and win people to Christ supposedly since their destiny has already been determined. Truly deadly doctrine.

There is Pentecostalism and its cheap false imitation of the gifts of the Spirit. Here we see the entrance into the church of the false spirits bringing so called tongues, ecstatic utterances, false prophecies etc. Simply spoken, since the modern Pentecostal tongues movement does not mirror the gift of tongues as it appeared in the N.T. church, it is void of truth and power. May God help the church to see this.

Also consider the false pre-trib escapism that Tim Lahaye and others have gained great wealth over promoting a false secret (secret as to timing for Christians) rapture escape from the anti-christ (all Christians of past centuries have been subject to the worst of all persecutions by anti-christ type figures, and so should **not** expect to be spared that in the future) when the true rapture takes place at the opening of the 6th seal, found in Revelation 6 , (which this seal ushers in the true wrath of God on earth, which no Christian will have to face.)

If students would compare the cosmic signs of Joel/Acts/Matthew 24 with those at the 6th seal (of Rev. ch.6) they would see that this seal ushers in the beginning of the "the day of the Lord" at which time yes, the elect or saved are raptured out , so as not to face this terrible time of wrath, "The great day of His wrath is come" Rev.6:17. Matthew 24 plainly shows that the "Gathering or snatching away of the elect" at the cosmic signs in this chapter is the same event which must therefore occur at the 6th seal, Revelation 6, where those same cosmic events take place

As in Noah's day, the wicked/unsaved will not be spared death after the Rapture, (the saved, having been gathered into the Ark is the "catching away") contrary to false Pre-Trib. claims. Will the wicked have a chance to be saved? NO! Rather they will come under the full wrath of God which is poured out after the opening of the 6th seal as the rapture is clearly happening at that point. *(Order this authors book available upon request: "The Infamous Rapture Conflict – Settled" which irrefutably proves the post-trib, pre wrath rapture. Order from, "Fundamental Baptist Publications, Eternity Publications. 1252 Sessions Rd. Elgin, S.C. 29045. $10.00 p.p.*

Jesus said…"And many false prophets shall rise, and shall deceive many". Matthew 24:11 "For there shall arise false Christ, and false prophets, and shall show great signs and wonders, insomuch that , if it were possible, they shall deceive the very elect" Matt 24:24

Be not carried about with divers and strange doctrines. For it is a good thing that the heart is established with grace; not with meats, which have not profited them that have been occupied therein. Hebrews 13:9

That we henceforth be no more children, tossed to and fro, and carried about with every wind of doctrine, by the sleight of men and cunning craftiness, whereby they lie in wait to deceive. Ephesians 4:14

AN INTERESTING HISTORICAL NOTE ON THE MODERN "TONGUES EXPERIENCE"

This author has written on the so called "tongues movement" some years ago. Recently I ran across a very interesting historical document which shows plainly that the cheap false imitation of the Bible's true gift of tongues that we see today in the Charismatic and Pentecostal Churches, was also manifested hundreds of years ago. The year was approximately 169 a.d. The book "Eusebius's Ecclesiastical History". We quote from page 171 and on.

"There is said to be a certain village of Mysia in Phrygia, called Ardaba. There, they say, one of those who was but a recent convert, Montanus by name, when Cratus was proconsul in Asia, in the excessive desire of his soul to take the lead, gave the adversary occasion against himself. So that he was carried away in spirit and wrought up into a certain kind of frenzy and irregular ecstasy, raving and speaking, and uttering strange things, and proclaiming what was contrary to the institutions that had prevailed modern in the church, as handed down and preserved in succession from the earliest times. (Here no doubt the "tongues" movement got it's start .ed.)

But of those that happened then to be present, and to hear these spurious oracles, some being indignant, rebuked him as one under the influence of demons and the spirit of delusion, and who was only exciting disturbances among the multitude. These bore in mind the distinction and the warning by our Lord, when he cautioned them to be vigilantly on their guard against false prophets. Others again, as if elated by the holy spirit, and gift of grace, and not a little puffed up, and forgetting the distinction made by our Lord challenged this insidious, flattering, and seducing spirit being themselves captivated and seduced by him; so that they could no longer restrain him to keep silence.

Thus, by an artifice, or rather by a certain crafty process, the devil having devised destruction against those that disobeyed the truth, and thus excessively honored by them, secretly stimulated and fired their understandings, already wrapped in insensibility, and wandering away from the truth. For he excited two others, females, and filled them with the spirit of delusion so that they also spake like the former, in a kind of ecstatic frenzy, out of all season, and in a manner strange and novel, while the spirit of evil congratulated, thus rejoicing and inflated by him and continued to puff them up the more, by promises of great things. Sometimes pointedly and deservedly, directly condemning them that he might appear also disposed to reprove them. Those few that were deceived were Phrygians, but the **same inflated spirit taught them to revile the whole church under heaven**, because it (the church ed.) gave neither access nor honor to this false spirit of prophecy, for when the faithful held frequent conservations in many places throughout Asia, for this very purpose and examined their novel doctrines and pronounced them vain and rejected them as heresy, then indeed they were expelled and prohibited from communication with the church." (Notice how easily the early church was susceptible to the embracing the entrance of heresy. ed.)

Conclusion

After relating these facts in the beginning of his work and introducing the refutation of their error in the body of the work he added the following remarks in the second book, respecting their end.

Therefore, said he, since they call us slayers of the prophets, saying "these were those whom the Lord promised to send to the people. Let them answer in the name of God, O friends, which of these who began prating from Montanus and his women, is there that suffered persecution, or was slain by the evil doers? None. Not one of their women was ever scourged in the synagogues of the Jews, or stoned, No, never.

"Montanus and Maximilla indeed, are said to have died another death than this, for at the instigation of that mischievous spirit, the report is that both of them hung themselves, not indeed at the same time, but at the particular time of each one's death, as the general report is; and thus they died terminated their life like the traitior Judas.

Thus also the general opinion is that, Theodotus, one of the first that was carried away by their prophecy as it was called and who became a kind of patron of the delusion, as if he should at some time be taken up and received into the heavens, and who falling into trances gave himself up to the spirit of deception, was finally tossed by him like a quoit into the air, and thus miserably perished. They say this happened as we have stated.

But, my friend we do not presume to know anything certain of these matters, unless we had seen them, for perhaps both Montanus and Theodotus and the above mentioned woman may have died in this way, or they may not."

He mentioned also in the same book that the holy Bishops of that time attempted to refute the spirit in Maximilla but were prevented by others who manifestly cooperated with the spirit.

His statement was as follows. "Let not, as is said in the same work of Asterius Urbanus, let not the spirit of Maximilla say, 'I am chased like a wolf from the flock, I am no wolf. I am utterance, spirit and power.' But let him show the power in the spirit effectually, and prove it. And let him by the spirit face those that were present at the time, to examine and argue with the babbling spirit, men who were eminent, and bishops of the church, Zoticus of Comana, Julian of Apamea whose tongues the followers of Themison bridled and prevented them from refuting the false and seducing spirit."

www.ingramcontent.com/pod-product-compliance
Lightning Source LLC
Chambersburg PA
CBHW021108080526
44587CB00010B/444